BRAVEHEARTS │ MEN IN SKIRTS

BRAVEHEARTS | MEN IN SKIRTS
ANDREW BOLTON

V&A PUBLICATIONS
DISTRIBUTED BY
HARRY N. ABRAMS, INC PUBLISHERS

First published by
V&A Publications, 2003

V&A Publications
160 Brompton Road
London SW3 1HW

Distributed in North America by
Harry N. Abrams, Incorporated,
New York

Designed by johnson banks

ISBN 0-8109-6591-7
(Harry N. Abrams, Inc)

Library of Congress Control Number
2001095100

Front jacket illustration: **Jean Paul Gaultier,
Autumn/Winter 2001–2**
Photograph courtesy of Donna Francesca

Back jacket illustration: **Jigsaw Menswear
advertising campaign, Autumn/Winter 1998–9**
Photograph courtesy of Terry Richardson
and Jigsaw Menswear

Frontispiece: **Jean Paul Gaultier,
Autumn/Winter 1985–6**
Photograph courtesy of Paolo Roversi/Streeters

Overleaf: **Dries Van Noten, Spring/Summer 2000**
Photograph by Takay for *Spoon*, 2000
Styled by Darryl Rodrigues
Courtesy of Takay and *Spoon*

Originated, printed and bound in Great Britain
by Butler & Tanner, Frome

HARRY N. ABRAMS, Inc
100 Fifth Avenue
New York, N.Y. 10011
www.abramsbooks.com

CONTENTS

ACKNOWLEDGEMENTS

There are many people who have been generous in their advice and support of this book and accompanying exhibition. In particular, I am indebted to: Philippe de Montebello, Director of The Metropolitan Museum of Art; Harold Koda, Curator in Charge of The Costume Institute at The Metropolitan Museum of Art; Carolyn Sargentson, Head of Research at The Victoria & Albert Museum; Sandra Holtby, Head of College at the London College of Fashion and Anna Wintour, Editor in Chief of American Vogue.

I would also like to extend my special thanks to:

My colleagues at The Costume Institute of The Metropolitan Museum of Art: Shannon Bell; Valerie Boisseau-Tulloch; Beth Dincuff Charleston; Michael Downer; Lisa Faibish; Joyce Fung; Charles Hansen; Stéphane Houy-Towner; Jessa Krick; Bernice Kwok-Gabel; Maya Naunton; Tatyana Pakhladzhyan; Chris Paulocik; Jessica Regan; Laurie Riley; Elyssa Schram Da Cruz; Lita Semerad; Melinda Webber Kerstein; Karen Willis; and the Docents.

My colleagues at The Metropolitan Museum of Art: Pamela T. Barr; Lisa Cain; Clint Coller; Deanna Cross; Jeff Daly; Joyce Denney; Giovanna Fiorino-Iannace; Toma Fichter; Christine Giuntini; Harold Holzer; Eric Kjellgren; Marilyn Jensen; Alisa LaGamma; Kerstin Larsen; Michael Langley; Rich Lichte; Elizabeth J. Milleker; Taylor Miller; Mark Morosse; John P. O'Neill; Doralynn Pines; Diana Pitt; Emily Rafferty; Gwen Roginsky; Patricia Sclater-Booth; Christine Scornavacca; Linda Sylling; Elyse Topalian; Valerie Troyansky; Daniel Walker and Barbara Weiss.

My former colleagues at the Victoria & Albert Museum: Ariane Bankes; Mary Butler; Albertina Cogram; Shaun Cole; Rosemary Crill; Debra Isaac; Anna Jackson; Nina Jacobson; Suzanne Lussier; Noreen Marshall; Susan North; Linda Parry; Susan Prichard; Margaret Scott; Suzanne Smith; Sonnet Stanfill; Marketa Uhlirova; Rebecca Ward; Alicia Weisberg-Roberts and Monica Woods.

My former colleagues at the London College of Fashion: Christopher Breward; Heather Lambert; Robert Lutton; Alistair O'Neill; Roy Peach; Norma Starszokowna and Sarah Wilshaw.

The institutional lenders to the exhibition: American Museum of Natural History (Division of Anthropology); Angels (Film and Television Division); National Museums of Scotland; Resurrection; San Diego Historical Society; Smithsonian Institute (National Museum of American History); Sotheby's and Warner Brothers.

The private lenders to the exhibition: Mrs Nicola Bowery; David Bowie; Hamish Bowles; Boy George; Harlon Crow; Evan Dando; Paul Frecker; Courtney Love; Donovan Leitch; Axel Rose; Philip Sallon; Sandy Schreier; Mark Walsh and Adrian Young (No Doubt).

The book designers: Sarah Fullerton and Michael Johnson.

The photographers: John Akehurst; Brian Aris; Robyn Beech; Dave Bennett; Koto Bolofo; Ugo Camera; Jean-François Carly; Henri-Cartier-Bresson; Alex Cayley; Davide Cernuschi; Richard Croft; Sophie Delaporte; Wouter Deruytter; Steve Double; Larry Dunstan; Aldo Fallai; Farabola Foto; Patricia Faure; Frank Forcino; Donna Francesca; Hideki Fujii; Raoul Gatchalian; Donald Graham; Henry Grant; David Gwinnutt; Laziz Hamani; Dave Hogan; Lee Jenkins; Davy Jones; Nick Knight; Christophe Kutner; Marco Lanza; Peter Lavery; Marcus Leatherdale; Mark Lebon; Annie Leibovitz; Mike Masoni; Niall McInerney; Steven Meisel; Randall Mesdon; Jamie Morgan; Jeremy Murch; Harry Page; Irving Penn Studio; Jean-Marie Périer; Martin Philbey; Pat Pope; Terry Richardson; Derek Ridgers; Ebet Roberts; Michael Roberts; Paolo Roversi; Peter Sanders; Deb Servey; Ram Shergill; David Simon; Patrice Stable; Chris Steele-Perkins; Sheryl Stevoff; Dennis Stone; Charles Sweel; Takay; Juergen Teller; Mario Testino; Pascal Therme; Mike Thomas; John Tiberi; Etienne Tordoir; Mike Toth; Francesco Valentino; Maria Valentino; Inez van Lamsweerde & Vinoodh Matadin; Albert Watson; Hywell Williams and Geoff Wilkinson.

The designers: 21st Century Kilts; Miguel Adrover; AmeriKilt; Amok; Giorgio Armani; As Four; John Bartlett; Ozwald Boateng; Bodymap; Burberry; Jean-Charles de Castelbajac; Roberto Cavalli; Clone Zone; Comme des Garçons; Christian Dior Haute Couture; Dolce & Gabbana; Philip Dubuc; Jacques Esterel; John Galliano; Jean Paul Gaultier; Rudi Gernreich; Marithé & Françoise Girbaud; Jeff Griffin; Gucci Group; Tommy Hilfiger; Jigsaw Menswear; Joe Kagan; Donna Karen New York; Kenzo; Michiko Koshino; Ralph Lauren; Maharishi; Antonio Marras; Masaki Matsushima; Alexander McQueen; Menintime; MIDAS; Daniel Moloney; Moschino Couture; Thierry Mugler; Kostas Murkudis; Tony Phillips; Carlo Pignatelli; Pringle of Scotland; John Richmond; Scotch House; Shirtology; Raf Simons; Hedi Slimane; Paul Smith; Luciano Soprani; Anna Sui; Utilikilts; Walter van Beirendonck; Gianni and Donatella Versace; Vivienne Westwood; Yohji Yamamoto and YSL – Rive Gauche.

Special thanks are also due to: Christine Arnold; Rebecca Arnold; Mickey Boardman; Harry and Marion Bolton; Elizabeth Bogner; Hugh Cheape; Adrian Clark; Judith Clark; Caroline Evans; Mattiebelle Gittinger; Tina Hammond; Marianna Klaiman; Mitzi Lorenz; Alice Percival; Barbara A. Porter; Patricia and Christopher Thomson and David Vincent.

SPONSOR'S STATEMENT

It is a great pleasure and an honor for Jean Paul Gaultier to participate in the exhibition "Bravehearts: Men in Skirts" organized by The Metropolitan Museum of Art's Costume Institute.

As a couturier, I have had the opportunity to attend several Costume Institute exhibitions. These exhibitions have had a significant influence on my work in regard to the relevance of the themes evoked and the richness of the pieces presented.

Now The Metropolitan Museum of Art with a liberal and open-minded perspective dedicates their exhibition to a theme I feel very strongly about: "Men in Skirts."

The skirt for a man is emblematic of the Jean Paul Gaultier wardrobe. Considering my work, convictions, and commitment, it was my duty to support such an initiative.

In my mind the prestige of The Metropolitan Museum of Art's Costume Institute, whose public is wide and diverse, will help the skirt to become a unisex item of clothing with cultural and historical realities once again. As a result of this exhibition, our western society will perhaps accept that men wear skirts, just as forty years ago it was accepted that women would wear trousers.

—Jean Paul Gaultier

INTRODUCTION

'A woman shall not wear anything that pertains to a man, nor shall a man put on a woman's garment; for whoever does these things is an abomination to the Lord your God.'
Deuteronomy 22.5

Throughout the history of Western dress, women have frequently borrowed elements of men's clothing. In the late sixteenth century, aristocratic women adopted men's hats and doublets, while in the late seventeenth and early eighteenth centuries they appropriated men's formal jackets (in both instances for riding, hunting or outdoor exercise). More recently, in the early twentieth century, fashionable women adopted men's trousers, an idea that was promoted by Amelia Bloomer as early as the 1850s. Examples of men appropriating women's dress, however, are far more rare. Since the Great Masculine Renunciation of the late eighteenth and early nineteenth centuries men have tended to follow a restricted code of dress. From the 1960s, with the rise of counter-cultures and an increase in informality, men have enjoyed more sartorial freedom, but they still lack access to the full repertoire of clothing worn by women. Today, while women enjoy most of the advantages of a man's wardrobe, men enjoy few of the advantages of a woman's wardrobe. Nowhere is this asymmetry more apparent than in the taboo surrounding men in skirts.

This book looks at designers as well as individuals who have appropriated the skirt as a means of injecting novelty into male fashion, as a means of transgressing moral and social codes, and as a means of re-defining ideal masculinities. As with trousers for women, there are crusading groups and individuals who wish to urge the practical benefits or advantages of the non-bifurcated garment. The results can be very much like bloomers, garments that are neither one thing nor the other. But the most striking skirts for men challenge the accepted commonsense of the clothes we wear. The continuing charge and social relevance of men wearing skirts comes out of the contentiousness of the act, the flaunting of the convention.

The term 'skirt' is used to refer to any 'non-bifurcated' garment, that is to say, any garment that is not divided down the middle below the waist. Where relevant, garments that look or function like skirts are examined, but true dress and skirt forms are the focus of the book. Generally speaking, we are not concerned with drag, transvestism or cross-dressing. This is because these are strategies primarily used for the exploration and construction of camp and feminine identities. Whilst this has a definite bearing on men in skirts, and their reception by society at large, this book is primarily concerned with the construction of masculine identities. By wearing skirts and posing style statements that challenge traditional notions of gender, skirts for men often pose similar questions to drag, but they have their own distinctive strategies, connections and associations. As the Belgian designer Dries Van Noten comments, 'There are the same differences between a man's and a woman's skirt as there are between a man and a woman.'

The book begins by examining the ways in which the skirt has been promoted as a utopian ideal and contemporary lifestyle decision. Through exploring the types and styles of skirts worn by men throughout history, it shows how recently men have lost their skirts and, at the same time, points to the historical bases of many recent skirt designs. An examination of skirts worn by men in Asia, Africa and the Middle East reveals that articles of clothing are not inherently male or female, masculine or feminine. By looking at a variety of non-Western skirted garments, the role of exoticism is explored in relation to the popularization and legitimization of the male skirt in the West. Exoticism and historicism come together in a study of the kilt, an item that has proved to be one of the most potent, versatile and wearable skirt forms. The book concludes by following the kilt and other skirted garments into the youth and subcultures of the late twentieth century, groups or movements for whom, in each of their separate ways, the skirt became a powerful means of transgression and self-expression. In the past as in the present, widespread acceptance of the skirt for men waits just over the horizon. Whether as threat or promise, it never fails to intrigue and provoke.

Jean Paul Gaultier, Autumn/Winter 1985–6
Photograph courtesy of Paolo Roversi/Streeters

MEN AGAINST TROUSER TYRANNY

The male skirt is always on the verge of arrival or widespread acceptance. Whether in the near future of 'next season' or in the distant future of 'Utopia', its status is always 'pending'. Since the late eighteenth century, certain groups and individuals have seen the skirt as the natural covering that would be left when we lost or gave up our cultural baggage. Typically, they have located the wearing of skirted or non-bifurcated garments in an edenic society in which gender distinctions have been obviated and unisex clothing is the norm. Many designers and stylists have been inspired by this fluid, futuristic construction of masculinity to envision the skirt as an extremity never to be reached, a shock at the edge of fashion that never loses its potency. The perpetual revolution of fashion could be maintained by the skirt's perceived unwearability and the threat (or temptation) of censure. For some men, however, a more egalitarian future of the global, instantaneous internet has already arrived. They are living and buying a skirt-wearing lifestyle today. At the confluence of novelty and reform, the idea of the skirt for men has come to be both the *ne plus ultra* of the catwalk and a highstreet lifestyle marketing tool.

Jacques-Louis David, *Le Citoyen Français*
Watercolour, 1794
Courtesy of Réunion des Musées Nationaux/
Art Resource, NY

THE FRENCH REVOLUTION

In 1770, the French writer and dramatist Louis-Sébastien Mercier wrote the utopian travelogue *L'An 2440*. Considered the first popular book set in the future, he describes the twenty-fifth-century Parisian as wearing a skirted or non-bifurcated costume in the form of a loose-fitting tunic fastening with a sash. Nineteen years later, Mercier's vision of the ideal dress of the future was re-visited by the various dress reformers of the French Revolution (1789-94). From the beginning of the Revolution, much thought was given to the reform of dress and how far appearances should contribute to the concept of equality.[1] Extravagance in dress was considered one of the most tangible expressions of the *ancien régime* and, therefore, an affront to patriotism and republican sympathies.[2] Luxury and formality gave way to simplicity and

informality. True patriots adopted the rough clothing and slovenly appearance of the *sans culottes*, a group of militant revolutionaries largely comprised of traders, craftsmen and shopkeepers. The *sans culottes* took their name from their refusal to wear knee-breeches (*culottes* or knee-breeches being identified with the aristocracy during the Revolution). Their costume was based on the typical working-class dress of the eighteenth century and included loose baggy trousers (*le pantalon*), a short boxy jacket (*le carmagnole*) and a pair of wooden shoes (*sabots*).

After the founding of the National Convention in September 1792, politicians and academicians began discussing the need to reform civilian dress to reflect republican morals and revolutionary character. In April 1794, the *Société Populaire et Républicaine des Arts* published a pamphlet entitled

Considérations sur la nécéssité de changer le costume français', advocating the reform of French dress based on a concern for liberty and equality as well aesthetics. Anticipating the concerns of the Men's Dress Reform Movement of the 1930s, the *Société Populaire et Républicaine des Arts* associated the idea of dress with physical well-being, 'In clothes better conceived than ours, men will become healthier, stronger, more agile, better able to defend their freedom.'[3] Copies of the *Considérations sur la nécéssité de changer le costume français* were submitted to the Convention and, in May 1794, the Comité de Salut Public contacted Jacques-Louis David to submit designs for both official and civilian costume.

One of the foremost artists of the Revolution, David's interest in costume, particularly classical costume, was well-known. During the Revolution the austere style

of neo-classicism permeated public life. As Aileen Ribeiro observes in *Fashion in the French Revolution* (1989), 'Classicism was linked with Jacobinism; grand, noble and terrible ideals on a large scale were the order of the day, forcing the last vestiges of the old, self-indulgent, princely rococo art forms underground.'[4] David's paintings and the *fêtes* he directed for the state drew on this sublime rhetoric. In what was perhaps his most spectacular festival, *Fête de l'Etre Suprême,* many of the male participants were dressed in what has been described as 'Roman' dress. David also designed the classical costumes for the actor Talma, teaching him the art of drapery.

While it is impossible to know if David had read Louis-Sébastien Mercier's prophetic *L'An 2440*, the designs he submitted to the Comité de Salut Public were remarkably similar to Mercier's dress of the future. The common denominator was a loose mantle, a tunic belted with a sash, tight-fitting pants, short boots or buskins, and a feathered *toque* trimmed with a cockade (above left). While the designs were a mixture of Classical, Medieval and Renaissance styles, they nevertheless revealed the 1790s aesthetic of emphasizing the shape of the body. The legs, in particular, became a focus of display, the tight-fitting pants suggesting a heroic nudity *à la romaine*.[5] The Comité de Salut Public instructed David to have thousands of his designs engraved and those for civilian costume to be distributed around the country where it was hoped they would be adopted by leading citizens.[6] However, his designs seem to have been adopted only by a few of the artist's friends and a coterie of his students, before the Jacobin government was overthrown in July 1794. Amid general unrest, the idea of a national dress for civilians was quickly abandoned.

In 1795, however, the new Directory government again considered the question of dress reform. While the idea of a national dress for civilians had proved unfeasible, 'the authorities continued to believe that some form of official costume was necessary to demonstrate the revolutionary cause in the face of a largely hostile world.'[7] The artist Jacques Grasset de Saint-Sauveur was given the task of designing a set of official costumes. These were published under the title *Costumes des Représentans du Peuple Français* in 1796. Like David, Grasset de Saint-Sauveur drew heavily on the costumes of classical antiquity, although there was a new emphasis on luxury. As Ribeiro explains, 'the new Directory, while wishing to distance itself from the excesses of the Jacobin regime

opposite: Eric Gill, engraving from *Clothes* (1931)
Courtesy of Irene Lewisohn Costume
Reference Library

and at the same time honouring the ideals of republicanism, nevertheless
believed that lavish official costumes would add lustre to the new
government, and to France.'[8]

Grasset's designs for members of the executive body were the
most extravagant, consisting of a short open coat (habit-manteau)
embroidered in gold, a double-breasted tunic also embroidered in gold
and tied with a sash, silk pantaloons, and a hat with tricolor panache.
Members of the legislative body wore long robes and mantles, 'a reminder
that in ancient Rome dignity was equated with ample draperies.'[9]
(page 13) While many people considered Grasset's designs to be pompous
and rather ridiculous, they were seen to represent the glory and power
of France. Since this was a primary concern of Napoleon, elaborate
official uniforms to distinguish those in authority continued to be devised
after the collapse of the Directory in 1799.

MEN'S DRESS REFORM PARTY

Physical welfare, rather than stately pomp, was the primary concern of the
Men's Dress Reform Party (MDRP), active in Britain during the 1930s.
While sharing some of the social and medical concerns of the various dress
reform groups of the late nineteenth century, the MDRP dwelt less on
aesthetics and the problems which beset workers in the clothing and allied
trades.[10] The more important incentives for the MDRP's reforms were 'fears
of the threat of feminism, class conflict, and imperial weakness.'[11] Barbara
Burman in her article 'Better and Brighter Clothes: The Men's Dress Reform
Party, 1929-1940' (1995) argues that the MDRP was heavily 'tinged by
eugenics and vestiges of the nineteenth-century Simple Life philosophy.'[12]

From the outset, however, the MDRP was committed to improving
men's dress in terms of health and appearance. It received much support
from the New Health Society, an organization which campaigned for
better awareness of the role of exercise, fresh air and good diet in improving
the health of adults and children. In fact, Dr Alfred Charles Jordan, one
of the co-founders of the New Health Society, was the MDRP's Honorary
Secretary. The Chairman of the Council was Dr Caleb Saleeby, founder
of the Sunlight League, an organization which promoted the benefits of air
and sunlight and one which also supported the MDRP. Upon its
founding in 1929, the MDRP's first act was to set up a design committee.
The introduction to its first report revealed the MDRP's position: 'Men's
dress has sunk into a rut of ugliness and unhealthiness from which – by
common consent – it should be rescued... Men's dress is ugly,
uncomfortable, dirty (because unwashable), unhealthy (because heavy,
tight and unventilated)... Only through wider individual choice and
variation will men's clothes be capable of healthy evolution and reasonable
adaptation to progressive social, hygienic and aesthetic ideals... All change
should aim at improvement in appearance, hygiene, comfort and convenience.'[13]

The MDRP promoted the wearing of fewer, looser fitting clothes
made from light, washable fabrics such as artificial silk. It advocated the
wearing of 'holiday' styles, such as soft open-necked shirts, for work
and city life. One of the Party's highest priorities was the abolition
of trousers, promoting shorts, breeches and kilts as alternatives. Its ideal
outfit consisted of 'shirts of rayon or fine poplin; jackets-and-shorts suits
(or jackets-and-kilt suits) of fine worsted or cashmere; good stockings
to match.'[14] Kilts met the sartorial objectives of the MDRP perfectly, offering
their wearers a veritable 'air bath'. Kilts had been proposed earlier in
New Health (1927), the monthly journal published by the New Health
Society. The writer advocated that all English boys should wear the kilt
on the grounds that it was the most hygienic and healthiest garment,
in addition to being 'easily the most becoming of all boys' wear.'[15]

Certain members of the MDRP did adopt skirted or non-bifurcated
garments. Dr Jordan, for example, was photographed wearing a
medieval-style tunic. In the *Tailor and Cutter* in July 1931, another reformer
was pictured sporting a short belted dress, resembling a smock. Such
images, however, served as weapons for the MDRP's opponents who
regarded its members as part of the 'loony fringe'. Skirted garments not
only bought the wearer's sexuality into question, but they also exposed
him to ridicule (as, indeed, might the lack of 'well-turned' calves, a source
of anxiety for many men).

The artist Eric Gill, a supporter of the MDRP, promoted skirts for
men in *Clothes: An Essay Upon the Nature and Significance of the Natural
and Artificial Integuments Worn by Men and Women* (1931). Gill argued
for an obliteration of the differences between men's and women's clothing
(opposite). After weighing up the pros and cons of whether both sexes

should wear skirts or trousers, he settled on skirts since 'It is essentially the garment of dignity, and dignity is the essential object of clothes.'[16] He qualified his decision by stating that men should not wear exactly the same clothes as women because, 'However similar in general arrangement men's bodies are to women's, there is sufficient difference, as, for example, in proportionate width of hips and shoulders and circumference of waist, between men and women to make fitting impossible.'[17] Gill realized, however, that before men (and women) would accept the notion of wearing skirts, 'men, that is to say Englishmen, European men and all so-called civilized men have to rid themselves of the preposterous notions that trousers are specially a male garment, and that skirts are specifically for women.'[18]

Perhaps encouraged by Gill's cogitations, the American designer Elizabeth Hawes created a 'fine flowing Arabian Nights robe'[19] for a fashion show in 1937. Commenting on her design in *Fashion is Spinach* (1938), Hawes exclaims, 'It made me quite certain, once and for all, that for being alluring, the skirt is the thing and there is no difference between the sexes.'[20] By the time she released her sequel to *Fashion is Spinach*, entitled *It's Still Spinach* (1954), Hawes was more emphatic about the skirt as the future of menswear. Referencing the MDRP's concerns, she proclaims:

'The sheiks of Araby, whose sexual exploits are legendary, wore skirts and they have never been considered sissies, to put it mildly. The American male is not only uncomfortable in his suits, but he has deprived himself of practically all the pleasures to be had from wearing colors, the feel of certain textures on his skin, the wind blowing on his body through his clothes, the sun and wind directly

on his body, or parts of it. That our men are not allowed to satisfy their souls in such simple human ways is a terrible thing.'[21]

MODERN MEN'S DRESS REFORM

In the late 1990s, various specialized groups were established to promote the social and medical benefits of the male skirt, taking over the MDRP's mantle of reform. Most of these groups, like 'Fashion Freedom' and 'The International Men's Fashion Freedom Network', have an internet presence. One of the more interesting sites is 'Bravehearts Against Trouser Tyranny' (BATT). Its aim is to 'liberate men from the "tyranny of trousers" that has been imposed upon us by Western society' and to 'encourage and promote the wearing, acceptance, and availability of kilts and other unbifurcated garments for men.'[22] Like many other special interest groups, BATT focuses on health, comfort and practicality, claiming that skirts are more suited to the male anatomy than trousers and that they liberate men from conventional male and masculine stereotypes. BATT also seeks to redress the inequality between men and women, maintaining that while women have a choice in whether to wear skirts or trousers, this choice is denied men.

Just as the internet allowed men who wanted to wear skirts to organize online, so it also created a marketing and distribution network for businesses interested in manufacturing skirted or non-bifurcated garments. Certain companies focus their attention on the kilt exclusively, such as Amerikilt.™ Like Utilikilts, another crusading company urging the practical advantages of the kilt, Amerikilt™ emphasizes the masculinity and functionality of the kilt at the expense of most of its other formal qualities (below left). Proudly made in the

USA, the Amerikilt™ is offered in military colours: tan, black, olive green and tiger stripe camouflage. Its detailing is masculine, with a wide front apron that secures with six metal snaps, a Velcro® tab at the belt line, and a pocket-style sporran that clips onto 'D' rings. The Amerikilt™ website proclaims that 'An Amerikilt is a true man's garment, designed for individual, free-thinking self-confident men.'[23]

The British-based company MIDAS (Men in Dresses and Skirts) offers a wider selection of skirts for men, including a denim 'jeans style' skirt with a front fly zip. Such a detail recalls Eric Gill's observation that skirts for men must be adapted to meet the physical needs and requirements of their male wearers if they are to appeal to the fashion-conscious male. While MIDAS mainly offers knee-length skirts, the German-based company Menintime specializes in ankle- or floor-length

versions (opposite). Menintime makes skirts that are designed to be worn at the beach or in the nightclub. Another German-based company, Persus, sells mainly wraparound, ankle- or floor-length skirts exclusively as club wear.

Perhaps the most innovative company specializing in skirts is the Swiss-based AMOK. Sandra Kuratle, its creative director, trained at both the Zurich Academy of Arts and the Zurich School of Art and Design. Unlike the other companies, Kuratle creates seasonal collections with regular runway presentations (below right). All her collections still ask, however, 'Are you man enough to experience a new dimension in men's fashion?'[24] While Kuratle also uses the arguments of comfort and practicality, she focuses more on the skirt as an aesthetic garment: 'The skirt for men is more than a political statement: men wearing skirts are not only self-confident

left: **Kilts by Amerikilt™**, Veterans Stadium, Philadelphia, 2003
Courtesy of AmeriKilt.com

right: **Amok (Sandra Kuratle)**, Autumn/Winter 2002-2003
Photograph courtesy of Maria Valentino/MCV Photo

opposite: **Denim Skirt by Menintime**, Spring/Summer 2003
Photograph by Mike Masoni
Courtesy of Mike Masoni and Menintime

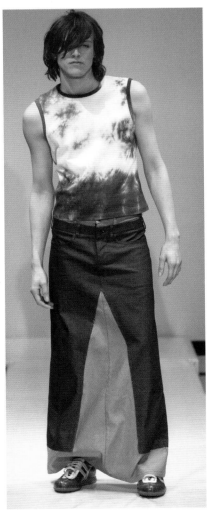

left: **Skirt suit by Jacques Esterel, 1966**
Courtesy of Jacques Esterel, Paris

top right: **Dress by Jacques Esterel,
'Negligé Snob' collection, 1970**
Courtesy of Jacques Esterel, Paris

bottom right: **Skirt suit by Jacques Esterel, 1966**
Courtesy of Jacques Esterel, Paris

opposite: **Jean Paul Gaultier, Spring/Summer 1985**
Photograph courtesy of Laziz Hamani

and courageous. In the first place they wear the skirt as a beautiful, fashionable and elegant garment, which will shape the future appearance of men beyond short-term trends.'[25]

SKIRTS À LA MODE

Skirts first entered the fashion system during the 1960s. Although perhaps best known for the pink and white gingham wedding dress he designed for Brigitte Bardot, the French couturier Jacques Esterel was one of the first designers to make a skirt for men. In 1966 he designed a 'skirt suit', comprising a jacket in grey, black and bordeaux check made from Dacron® (above left). Inspired by the Scottish kilt,

it was not in fact a skirt, but a pair of Bermuda shorts, one leg of which wrapped over the other. The design was later to inspire Jean Paul Gaultier, who created a longer version for his Spring/Summer 1985 collection 'And God Created Man' (right). Esterel's shorts, like Gaultier's trousers, gave the illusion of a skirt and sparked an explosion of commentary in the popular press. Journalists and cartoonists focused on the fear or danger of role reversal. This fear was all the more real at the time because many aspects of society, including the definitions of masculinity and femininity, were being questioned. Photographs of Esterel's design that appeared in various fashion

magazines at the time played on this fear. In one photograph, a man in the skirt suit is shown accepting a light from a woman in black leather trousers (above right). To emphasize the tension between 'a man in a skirt and a woman in a pair of trousers', the model is shown sporting the same hairstyle as his female counterpart, Vidal Sassoon's famous 'Five-point Cut.'

Later, in 1970, Jacques Esterel created a unisex robe (top). Unisex clothing is designed to suppress the conventions of masculine and feminine dress, privileging an androgynous body. As Rebecca Arnold argues in *Fashion, Desire and Anxiety: Image and Morality in the 20th Century* (2001), 'In the

twentieth century the fragmentation of traditional lines of status and power has led to periods when solace has been sought through this denial of difference. The diversity of contemporary culture and the break-up of existing ideas of gender, race and sexuality led to confusion surrounding definitions of identity.'[26] Most frequently, uncertainty surrounding gender identities has led to a simpler, more functional and more masculine way of dressing. Indeed, as Arnold points out, 'Although promising gender equality, unisex dress has always been essentially masculine in style.'[27] Esterel, however, was advocating unisex dress based on feminine styles.

This strategy was also employed by the British textile manufacturer Joe Kagan (right). In October 1966, he told the annual convention of the British Menswear Association that 'In the 1980s men will be wearing skirts or kilts like those worn by the ancient Roman soldiers.'[28] Four years later, Rudi Gernreich repeated Kagan's prediction, prophesying that by the year 2000, 'Clothing would not be identified as either male or female. So women will wear pants and men will wear skirts interchangeably.'[29] For the elderly he predicted boldly patterned caftans, since 'If a body can no longer be accentuated, it should be abstracted.' (opposite) Designs for young men and women included canary yellow mini-skirts, which appear in a photograph by Patricia Faure (right). As the photograph shows,

opposite page: **Unisex caftans by Rudi Gernreich, 1970**
Photograph courtesy of Hideki Fujii

above: **Skirt by Joe Kagan, 1966**
Courtesy of Syndication International/
Photo Trends ©Mirrorpix

right: **Unisex mini-skirts by Rudi Gernreich, 1970**
Photograph courtesy of Patricia Faure

however, Gernreich failed to 'exorcise traditional patterns of imagery from his vision of an egalitarian future. His man and woman may be dressed identically but posed in the familiar stances of angular, erect male and curving, submissive female.'[30]

In Walter van Beirendonck's Autumn/Winter 1999-2000 'No References' collection, Gernreich's prediction was realized in a series of mini skirts worn with latex body stockings (below left). Like Gernreich, van Beirendonck, whose logo is 'Fuck the Past (Kiss the Future)', is a highly visionary designer who uses fashion

(and particularly skirts) as a means of challenging traditional definitions of masculinity. Since the late 1980s, van Beirendonck has experimented with a variety of skirted garments. As well as minis, he has produced midis and maxis in plain and pleated styles. 'I have always found the skirt an intriguing garment', he explains. 'On a man, it is more than an item of clothing, it is a statement. I try to use the skirt in a "natural" way, not in a transgendered way. When it is properly balanced, a skirt is without gender. If only society was not so conditioned, then a skirt would be an essential item of a man's

wardrobe.'[31] Van Beirendonck explored the non-gender specificity of the skirted garment in greater depth in his Spring/Summer 2000 'Gender?' collection, which included crocheted dresses worn over floral cotton trousers (below right). In an interview with Suzy Menkes, van Beirendonck said of the collection, 'Whether clothes are for men and women is all in the head – and none of these are 100 percent.' It is a view shared by the American design company As Four, whose skirted garments, like those of van Beirendonck, question accepted or received notions of gendered clothing (opposite).

left: **Walter van Beirendonck, 'No References' collection, Autumn/Winter 1999–2000**
Photograph courtesy of Maria Valentino/MCV Photo

below: **Walter van Beirendonck, 'Gender?' collection, Spring/Summer 2000**
Photograph by Etienne Tordoir
Courtesy of Walter van Beirendonck

opposite: **Skirt by As Four, 2000**
Photograph courtesy of As Four and *zingmagazine*

left: Photograph by Mark Lebon for *i-D,* 1984
Styled by Ray Petri
Courtesy of Mark Lebon

right: Photograph by Mark Lebon for *i-D,* 1984
Styled by Ray Petri
Courtesy of Mark Lebon

opposite
left: Photograph by Jamie Morgan for *The Face,* 1984
Styled by Ray Petri
Courtesy of Jamie Morgan

right: Photograph by Mark Lebon, mid-1980s
Styled by Ray Petri
Courtesy of Mark Lebon

NEW MAN, NEW LAD AND THE METROSEXUAL

Trousers for women became acceptable largely because society re-assessed its definitions of women and femininity. Despite the efforts of reformers and designers to promote the skirt for men as a rational, practical and fundamentally aesthetic garment, skirts for men remain a taboo. For many men, their feminine connotations are too potent to overcome the fear that by wearing a skirt, their gender identity might be brought into question. Ultimately, men's roles in society as well as society's definitions of masculinity need to change before skirts become an acceptable alternative to trousers. In the mid-1980s, this seemed a possibility through the construction of new, differentiated forms of masculinity, most notably that of the 'new man'. The new man represented the non-sexist, post-feminist male who indulged in the pleasures of consumption. As Paul Jobling explains in *Fashion Spreads: Word and Image in Fashion Photography Since 1980* (1999), 'new man became common currency in media circles, if not in society at large, to describe the consumerist ethos of a certain constituency of British males

(arguably, white collar professionals, aged 18-35 years old).'[32] New man was not afraid to take an interest in his appearance or get in touch with his caring, nurturing side. Magazine stylists played a crucial role in promoting the image of the new man, perhaps the most notable being Ray Petri. His fashion stylings of men in skirts in the pages of *i-D* and *The Face* in the mid-1980s were the personification of the sensitive or, more accurately, 'enlightened' male. Produced under his trademark label 'Buffalo', these images were built by a close group of associates that included the stylist Mitzi Lorenz, the model Nick Kamen and the photographers Mark Lebon, Roger Charity, Jamie Morgan and Norman Watson.

At least in part, Petri's early stylings of men in skirts were inspired by Mark Lebon who started wearing waistcloths in London in the early 1980s.[33] As Lebon explains, 'I used to get them off my friend Yvonne Gold who used to bring them back from Africa. They were printed with the most amazingly modern designs such as boomboxes and cigarette packets. I also wore homemade sarongs. One I remember, in particular, was made from a blue European Union flag, which Ray loved.'[34] For one of his first photoshoots of men in

skirts, Petri used a 'prayer shawl' combined with a long, heavy woollen coat (above left). Photographed by Lebon with the model Nick Kamen, it appeared in *i-D* in July 1984 with the caption, 'The mood is reflective… The gesture of quiet confidence. It's a tribute to colour, fresh air and clean living. He's the intellectual pilgrim.'[35]

Debates in the popular press about new man allowed for the possibility of men in skirts. In Petri's stylings, this possibility involved striking the right balance between male and masculine and female and feminine. As Lebon comments, 'Although Ray's stylings of men in skirts were very theatrical, they were never effete or effeminate. Ray always tried to offset the feminine connotations of the skirt with masculine props or accessories. The look was not intended to threaten a man's masculinity, it was intended to enhance it.'[36] In one particular styling, which appeared in *i-D* in October 1984, Petri used a naval jacket to counterbalance the skirt's feminine overtones (above right). Not only does the jacket invoke the iconic, hyper-masculine status of the naval officer, but it also emphasizes and accentuates the model's broad, masculine frame. At the same time, the model's

clenched fists, assertive posture and expression present a tough, muscular image that is set off against an urban backdrop, highlighting the skirt's avant-garde metropolitanism. Although the hand-print skirt formed part of a woman's suit by Vivienne Westwood, in Petri's hands it has been re-contextalized as an essential element of masculine, urban streetstyle.

Through his stylings of men in skirts, Petri strove to masculinize the skirt in an attempt to promote the idea that masculinity is not attached to any particular garment. As Jamie Morgan comments, '[I] defy any stylist or photographer to take a picture of a guy wearing a skirt and make him look sexy but not stupid. That was Ray's power. His images were strong and sensitive – they showed you didn't have to drink beer and beat people up to be tough. He gave men a sense of pride in the way they dress which has been hugely influential.'[37] Central to this was his use of tough, well-built men with chiselled features, which, as Sean Nixon comments in *Hard Looks: Masculinities, Spectatorship & Contemporary Consumption* (1996), imbued the photoshoots he styled with 'a tough, muscular masculinity that drew tangentially on the representational genres of 1950s bodybuilding and boxing portraiture.'[38] Nixon also draws attention to the interplay of softness and hardness inherent in Petri's styling, seen clearly in a photograph by Lebon, in which the physical solidity of the model's torso is offset by the soft drape of the skirt's fabric (above right). The model's nakedness and provocative pose underscore the sexualization of the male skirt.

Petri's stylings in the pages of *i-D* and *The Face* in the mid-1980s served to increase the visibility and momentum of men in skirts. Perhaps his most famous and memorable stylings appeared in *The Face* in November 1984 (above left). They were photographed by Morgan using the models Nick Kamen and Camillo Gallardo to accompany an article written by Glenda Bailey on contemporary men's fashion entitled 'Men's Where?' The article argued that menswear was undergoing a revolution. In the 1980s, menswear increased significantly with the growth in retail of flexible specialization which allowed for greater market differentiation in products. Bailey wrote, 'Men's fashion is receiving more serious attention and exposure and its wearers are spending much more money.'[39] The article focused on a number of new, up-and-coming men's fashion designers and speculated on the future of menswear, presenting men in skirts as a possible way forward. The stylings presented by Petri were typically young, street and masculine. Like his photoshoots for *i-D*, he relied on a range of masculine props and accessories such as thick socks, heavy shoes and boots to promote a masculine aesthetic. However, as the cover of the issue boldly declared, men in skirts was 'menswear at the outer limits'. Bailey finished her piece by declaring, 'Still, the dissenting voices protest, things haven't changed that much: there's still no British equivalent of the influential men's fashion magazine *GQ*, still no male version of the Joseph empire and still no real men wearing skirts.'[40] The fact that men in skirts was seen as the extremity of men's fashion was confirmed by Nick Logan when he set up *Arena* in 1986. He stated, 'The fashion was crucial – to attract, and not scare off, both readers and advertisers there was no place in *Arena* for Men In Skirts.'[41]

Definitions of masculinity changed in the 1990s with the emergence of the 'new lad',

Kenny Logan in a kilt by Dries Van Noten
Photograph by Jean-François Carly for *GQ*, 2000
Styled by Jo Levin
Courtesy of Jean-François Carly

overleaf: **Comme des Garçons,
Autumn/Winter 1998–9**
Photograph by Mike Thomas for
Arena Homme Plus, 1998
Courtesy of Mike Thomas

a reaction to the new man. As Tim Edwards explains in *Men in the Mirror: Men's Fashion, Masculinity and Consumer Society* (1997), 'Where the New Man was caring and sharing, if overly concerned with the cut of his Calvin Kleins, the New Lad is selfish, loutish and inconsiderate to a point of infantile smelliness. He likes drinking, football and fucking and in that order of preference.'[42] New lad was promoted through magazines such as *FHM, Maxim* and *Loaded* and television programmes such as *Men Behaving Badly*, a British sitcom 'stuffed full of jokes about drunkenness, football and men's untidiness.'[43] Revelling in 'shagging and beer swilling', the new lad proudly wore his undiluted misogyny and (often affected) working-class machismo on his sleeve.[44]

Despite new lad's defensive masculinity, skirts continued to play a role in the promotion of new laddism. In a photograph by Jean-François Carly, the stylist presents new lad (in the body of Kenny Logan who plays left wing for the London Wasps) wearing a kilt, the new lad skirt par excellence (left). Paired with a T-shirt and accessorized with a rugby ball, his new lad status is both undeniable and unquestionable. For many editorial presentations of the new lad, sport is often used to normalize the wearing of skirts, drawing, as it does, on the language of 'loutishness'. In another photograph by Mike Thomas, the skirt-wearing new lad is presented 'out with the boys' in the hyper-masculine context of the pub (pages 28–9). Propping up the bar, they gaze off into the distance with a predatory look, the implication being that they are 'checking out a babe'. Far from presenting an image of self-conscious dishevelment, however, the gang of new lads are no less well-groomed than their predecessors. Herein lies the irony, for there is as much continuity as there is change in the development of new laddism.[45] The new lad, like his non-sexist, post-feminist counterpart new man, was firmly located within the feminine world of consumption. As Edwards argues, 'If the New Man sold muscles and scent, Armani and Calvin Klein, then the New Lad sells T-shirts and trainers, Hugo by Hugo Boss and Prada… the styles may have altered, yet the drive to consume remains the same.'[46]

Men Against Trouser Tyranny   29

Whereas new lad was 'a rather schizoid fellow',[47] the metrosexual, a new type of masculine identity that emerged in the late 1990s, combines the traits of new man and new lad effortlessly. Described as '[a] straight urban [man] willing, even eager, to embrace [his] feminine [side]',[48] the metrosexual, despite emerging as a term in the mid-1990s to satirize consumerism's toll on traditional masculinity, has become a media phenomenon firmly located in consumer culture. In his article 'Metrosexuals Come Out' (2003), Warren St John presents the British footballer David Beckham as a metrosexual icon, a man who 'paints his fingernails, braids his hair and poses for gay magazines, all while maintaining a manly profile on the pitch.'[49] Beckham's metrosexual iconic status was confirmed when he wore a sarong

by Jean Paul Gaultier in the South of France in 1998 (below). As Beckham explains in his biography *Beckham My World* (2000):

'Victoria has never told me what to wear. Obviously, she buys things for me, but I bought the infamous sarong when I was out with Mel B's ex-husband, Jimmy, in Paris. In fact, I liked it so much, I bought several in different colours and Jimmy bought a couple as well. Jimmy was great to go shopping with because he knew where all the good shops were and he was one of the coolest male dressers I've ever met. So buying the sarong had nothing to do with Victoria. There were probably loads of people out there thinking, what's a man doing in a sarong. What's going through his head? She's wearing the trousers and she's got him wearing a skirt. But some people

with broader minds must have thought, well, he looks good in it, so what's the problem? Unfortunately, there aren't enough open-minded people thinking that way.'[50]

Beckham's adoption of the skirt did much to promote its acceptance among fellow metrosexuals. Paradoxically, however, it also encouraged the trend among British football fans to wrap the St George or Union Jack flag around their waists. Despite the resemblance to a sarong, such a demonstration of patriotism often carries uneasy associations with a defiantly masculine political extremism. This association, however, has not prevented stylists from drawing upon such imagery in their efforts to promote the skirt as a viable and practical alternative to trousers in the pages of men's fashion magazines (right).

David Beckham in a sarong by Jean Paul Gaultier, Nice, France, 1998
Photograph by Harry Page ©News International

opposite: **Photograph by Jamie Morgan for** *i-D*, 2001
Styled by Mitzi Lorenz
Courtesy of Jamie Morgan

SKIRTS IN HISTORY

While today skirted or non-bifurcated garments are primarily associated with women, throughout the history of Western dress they have been worn by both men and women and have served to signify both masculinity and femininity. Until the fourteenth century, men and women tended to wear skirted garments that were similar in terms of cut and construction. This does not mean, however, that dress failed to differentiate between the sexes. The sex of the wearer might still be determined by the length, colour, decoration and arrangement of a garment. If men flouted these conventions, they were often criticized on the grounds of immodesty and, more pointedly, effeminacy. After the fourteenth century, when men's garments essentially became bifurcated as a consequence of the evolution of tailoring techniques, men did not immediately stop wearing non-bifurcated garments. Until the beginning of the twentieth century, men continued to wear skirted garments in the form of robes, gowns and full-skirted coats.

SKIRTS

In the history of Western dress, skirts, in the form of an animal skin or length of material wrapped around the waist or hips, were among the earliest forms of clothing. Men in the ancient Middle Eastern culture of Sumer, for instance, wrapped long-haired goat- and sheep-skins around their waists. Known as *kaunakès*, they were usually calf-length and generally belted or girdled at the waist. Later, woven textiles, often fringed at the hem or made to imitate goat- and sheep-skin, were worn wrapped around the waist in the same manner.

While wrapping provided the most basic skirt form in many civilizations of antiquity, it was not necessarily a simple style. In ancient Egypt, men wore a variety of skirts created by complex forms of drapery. One style was starched at the front so that the bottom hem extended forwards to form a rigid and somewhat unwieldy triangular projection (above). Made from linen and frequently pleated, it was worn by high officials in the Old Kingdom (2649–2150 BCE) and, in a more modest form, in the Middle Kingdom (2040–1640 BCE).

Egyptian men also wore skirts with separate aprons, the best-known example being the *shendyt*, a style that was reserved almost exclusively for the Pharaoh in the Old Kingdom.[1] In relief and statuary, this style is represented as a short wraparound skirt with the two side edges curving symmetrically from the centre of the waistband to the outer edges of the thighs (opposite). Between the legs hangs a tapering apron, which gives the *shendyt* a tripartite effect in front view.

Another intricate style worn by men in ancient Egypt was the sash skirt. It appeared during the New Kingdom (1550–1070 BCE), a period when styles became fussier and more frivolous as a response to the demands of an expanding empire.[2] The sash skirt was formed from a length of pleated fabric wrapped around the hips and tied in front. The fabric was wrapped in such a way as to produce a high waistline at back and a concave or sagging waistline at front. One or both of the free ends hung down between the legs, sometimes revealing a fringed selvedge for

decorative effect. In relief and statuary, a variation of the sash skirt is represented with one end draped so as to create an elaborate scalloped effect. Often, the sash skirt was worn with other non-bifurcated garments like a short bag tunic.

Several contemporary designers have looked to the different styles of skirts worn by men in ancient Egypt for both inspiration and legitimization. The French designers Marithé & François Girbaud created a version for their Autumn/Winter 1988-9 collection (page 34). Constructed by wrapping a rectangular length of fabric around the hips, its printed, sunburst design of black and purple stripes was designed to emulate the elaborately pleated triangular skirt. It was an effect that was used also by the Italian designer Carlo Pignatelli in a skirt he designed for his Spring/Summer 1997 collection (page 34). With its curved edges and *trompe l'oeil* pleating, it was based on the *shendyt* style worn by the pharaoh in the Old Kingdom. Made from towelling, Pignatelli's design also referenced what is perhaps the most common and unconscious skirt form worn by men today, the towel.

TUNICS AND MANTLES

Like skirts, tunics were an essential item of male attire in most civilizations of antiquity. In terms of construction they varied over time and across cultures. A type known as the *chiton* was the principal garment for men in ancient Greece. Art and literary sources reveal a variety of different styles distinguished by their length, material and construction. In the Classical Period (540-400 BCE), there were two dominant styles: the so-called Ionic and Doric *chitons*. The Ionic *chiton*, which was the more complex and elaborate of the two, was popular in the earlier Classical Period. Typically, it was made from two rectangles of fabric, usually of linen, sewn together at either side-seam, from top to bottom, forming a tube or cylinder. Leaving apertures in the centre for the head and at either end for the arms, the top edges were gathered and sewn or pinned together to create shoulder-seams. Because of the width of the garment, these shoulder seams created 'false sleeves' of varying lengths when worn. A representation of the Ionic *chiton* with sewn shoulder seams can be seen in the fifth-century BCE bronze sculpture *Charioteer of*

Delphi in the Archaeological Museum of Delphi in Greece (right). The *chiton* falls to the ankles and is girdled at the waist forming a blouson known as the *kolpos*. Left un-girdled, the *chiton* would trail along the floor. Ordinarily, the girdle created a dolman-style drape to the underarm area but as the figure is a charioteer, this fullness is controlled by the addition of shoulder bands.

In relief and statuary, the shoulders of the Ionic *chiton* are often depicted as pinned at short intervals. This method of fastening created a fissured shoulder-line that is sometimes referred to as the 'Ionic sleeve'. It can be seen clearly on the figure of the Lydian King Croesus, as represented on a sixth–fifth century BCE Attic red-figure amphora attributed to Myson in the Louvre in Paris (below). Like the *chiton* represented in the *Charioteer of Delphi*, it is worn to the ankles. Typical of tunics worn by men in most civilizations of antiquity, the length of *chitons* usually reflected the age, status or occupation of the wearer. While the more dignified ankle-length *chiton* was generally associated with older and wealthier men, it was a style that was also worn by certain professions such as priests,

left: **Myson**, Attic red figure amphora, late 6th–early 5th century BCE
The Louvre, Paris
Courtesy of RMN/Art Resource, NY

opposite: *Charioteer of Delphi*
Bronze
Greek, 478 or 474 BCE
Archaeological Museum, Delphi
Courtesy of Erich Lessing/Art Resource, NY

actors, musicians and charioteers. By contrast, younger and less privileged men, as well as those involved in active pursuits such as warriors and workmen, wore a shorter, thigh-length version. As can be seen by the apparel of King Croesus' attendant, Euthymos, servants and labourers might wear a simple waistcloth or *zoma* in the form of a length of cloth wrapped around the hips or waist. Many other red-figure vases reveal that waistcloths or *zomata* could also be worn by athletes and craftsmen.

Over his Ionic *chiton*, King Croesus wears a cloak or mantle known as the *himation*. Since the Archaic Period (1100-540 BCE), it was common for men in Greece to wear cloaks over their *chitons*. In the *Iliad* King Agamemnon awakes in the morning and prepares to meet the assembly of the Achaeans:

'But rousing himself from sleep, the divine voice swirling round him,

Atrides sat up, bolt awake, pulled on a soft tunic, linen never worn, and over it threw his flaring battle-cape, under his smooth feet he fastened supple sandals, across his shoulder slung his silver-studded sword.' [3]

The *himation* was made from a wide rectangle of fabric, usually of wool, and varied in size depending on the status of the wearer. As Ethel Abrahams points out in *Greek Dress* (1964), there were definite points of etiquette involved in the correct draping of the *himation*. 'It was considered a mark of good breeding', she comments, 'to throw it over the shoulder and let it hang down in such a way as to cover the left arm completely. To wear it "over the left side" was a mark of boorishness, as we gather from Aristophane's *Birds*, where Poseidon taunts the barbarian Triballus for wearing it so.' [4] Similarly, to let the hem of the

himation trail on the floor was considered foppish and effeminate. [5]

After the Peloponnesian War (431-404 BCE), there was a reaction against the elaborate and luxurious dress of the early Classical Period. The Ionic *chiton* came to be associated with Eastern or, more precisely, Persian dress, and was rejected in favour of the Doric *chiton*, which was a Spartan style in every sense. The Doric *chiton* was made from a large rectangle of fabric, usually of wool, folded in half widthways and sewn up the side to form a tube or cylinder. It was fastened on the left and right shoulders by a *fibula* or brooch, the fabric being carried forward from behind and pinned at front. Instead of covering the arms, like the Ionic *chiton*, the fabric fell away from the *fibulae* to create a sleeveless garment. When belted at the waist, the Doric *chiton* usually reached to the knees. A variation of the Doric *chiton* was the *exomis*, which was constructed in the same way except that it was pinned at the left shoulder only, leaving the right arm entirely free (below right). It was a style that was usually worn by men engaged in strenuous activity, such as servants and labourers. In art, it is often worn by gods and heroes in action.

The juxtaposition of a bared chest with classical drapery is an image of male authority that has resonated through history. It is an image that later artists and designers have responded to when representing heroic dress. In art, one of the most famous examples is the statue of George Washington by the American artist Horatio Greenough (oppsite). Clad only in the *himation*, which Bernard Rudofsky described as 'locker-room négligé',[6] this large-scale monument aroused the wrath of a prurient nation when it was unveiled. As Greenhough himself put it, 'Purblind squeamishness awoke with a roar at the colossal nakedness of

Washington's manly breast'.[7] Rudofsky explains that the statue was intended to be placed beneath the vaulted arch of the Capitol, but was relegated to the grounds where it languished half hidden by shrubbery. Eventually, the ostracized work of art was granted asylum at Washington's Smithsonian Institution. In fashion, John Galliano, a designer well-known for drawing inspiration from the past, created a series of classically-inspired garments from deconstructed football jerseys for his Spring/Summer 2001 collection. In one piece, he draped the jersey from the right shoulder to form a garment that resembled the *exomis* (below left). Galliano often plays with notions of ideal masculinities, and in this piece he has combined the clothing style and iconography of a Greek God with that of a modern-day football hero.

Compared to the Greeks, the Romans were much more conservative regarding the exposure

of the body and disapproved of public nudity.[8] The basic garb of a Roman male was a tunic, in Latin called a *tunica*. Until the third century AD, two distinctive types of tunics, based on different methods of construction, were worn by men in ancient Rome. The first was made from two rectangles of fabric, usually of wool, sewn together at the top and sides. A horizontal opening was left at the top for the head and vertical openings were left at the sides for the arms. In the early Republic (509–27 BCE), this type of tunic was narrow and sleeveless, but in the last years of the Republic and the first two centuries of the Empire (31 BCE–AD 395), it was wider and had sleeves of varying lengths. These sleeves were 'false' sleeves, formed naturally by the width of the tunic. The second type of tunic was made from one rectangle of fabric folded over lengthways and sewn up the sides with apertures left for the arms. This tunic could be sleeveless or, as was

opposite: **Horatio Greenough**, *George Washington*, 1840
Courtesy of Smithsonian American Art Museum, Washington DC/Art Resource, NY

left: **John Galliano**, Spring/Summer 2001
Photograph by Patrice Stable
Courtesy of John Galliano

right: *Fallen Gaul*
Greek, 2nd century BCE
Museo Archeologico di Venezia
Courtesy of Alinari/Art Resource, NY

more often the case, it might have sleeves of varying lengths. These sleeves, however, were not made separately and sewn into the armholes but were woven, on a very wide loom, as part of the tunic. The neckline was also formed during the weaving process. When folded over along the shoulderline, the tunic was sewn up the sides and along the undersides of the sleeves.

For the Romans, dress primarily served to signify rank, status, office or authority.[9] Although tunics were worn by all men from slaves to Emperors, various conventions were employed for the immediate recognition of socio-economic differences, such as the colour and the quality of the cloth used. Whereas the tunics worn by upper-class men were made from fine-quality wool and were usually bleached white, those worn by lower-class men were made from coarser wool that was generally dark in colour, for example brown or yellow-orange, perhaps reflecting the natural colours of unbleached wool.[10] Among the upper classes, status or office was also demarcated by the width of two woven purple stripes, one passing over each shoulder and extending to the lower edge of the tunic, both front and back. A wider stripe known as the *latus clavus* was worn by the senatorial order, while a narrower stripe known as the *augustus clavus* was worn by the equestrian order.

In addition to the colour, quality and decoration of the cloth used, there were other sartorial conventions used to designate status. Describing the correct length of an orator's tunic in *The Orator's Education*, Quintilian insisted, 'A speaker who is not entitled to the Broad Stripe [of the senatorial order] should gird his tunic in such a way that its front edge falls a little below the knee, and the back edge reaches to the middle of the calf. Anything lower is for women; anything higher is for centurions.'[11] This last statement reveals that in ancient Rome, clothing was not only viewed as part of the outward arrangement of visualizing rank, but also as part of a moral system.[12]

The most culturally significant item of Roman costume, however, was the toga. This voluminous draped garment was crucial to Roman self-representation, and, as the Empire extended, became a visible symbol of Roman law, religious authority and family values throughout the Ancient World. Initially worn by both men and women, by the second century BCE it was restricted to adult males (girls until the age of 12, that is until puberty, however, were entitled to wear it). Furthermore, laws passed in the middle of the first century restricted its use to free-born male citizens. Slaves, exiles and foreigners were prohibited from wearing the toga lest they be mistaken for citizens.[13] Originally, the toga was worn by men without an undergarment except a loincloth or *subligaculum*, but by the second century BCE it was worn over a tunic. In theory, all free-born male citizens, regardless of their class or status, were entitled to wear the toga. However, in practice, those of lower rank, who had to work for a living, usually wore their togas only on holidays, that is, at religious festivities. For this reason, they were often referred to, more or less contemptuously, as the 'tunic-clad populace'.[14] The tunic worn under the toga was usually belted or girdled and always had short sleeves. From the late third and early fourth centuries, however, it became fashionable to wear two tunics of differing lengths under the toga.

Like the Greek *himation*, the toga was made from a length of fabric, generally white wool. But, unlike the *himation*, which was rectangular in shape, the toga was always at least half elliptical with rounded ends. Despite differences in size, shape and styles of draping, the basic method of wearing the toga was consistent throughout the Republic and the Empire. As Shelley Stone describes in 'The Toga: From National to Ceremonial Costume' (2001):

'First an entire side of the garment was loosely rolled into folds. One end of the side with these folds was placed against the lower left leg of the wearer, then passed up the left side and over the shoulder. The rest of the toga was then wrapped loosely around the back and placed beneath the right arm in order to facilitate the use of the arm. Then the remainder of the garment was brought around the chest and thrown back over the left shoulder, concealing the end of the toga from which the drapery started.'[15]

Since no pins or brooches were employed to secure the toga, the left arm was held against the side to hold the cloth in place on the left shoulder.

Consistent with their emphasis on depicting status through costume, the Romans evolved different forms of decoration to indicate precisely the rank or nature of the wearer. The toga worn by the Roman private citizen, called the *toga virilis*, was plain white. High priests and officials such as consuls and magistrates wore a toga which had a purple stripe approximately two to three inches in width along its border. Known as the *toga praetexta*, it was also worn by free-born boys until the age of 14 to 16, when they adopted the *toga virilis*. An example of the *toga praetexta* can be seen in the *Arringatore*, a bronze statue of an Etruscan municipal magistrate named Aule Meteli (Aulus Metellus). Dating to the early first century BCE, it clearly shows the stripe running along the lower border of the garment (page 40). The *toga candida*, an artificially whitened toga, was worn by candidates seeking office, and an all-purple toga was the privilege of the Emperor, although it was accorded to others on special occasions.

Perhaps because it was so crucial to the social and political definitions of citizenship and, therefore, masculinity in the Roman Empire, the toga has often been a source of inspiration for contemporary designers. Vivienne Westwood has produced several dresses for men based on the Roman toga. These 'toga dresses' first appeared in Westwood's Autumn/Winter 1982-3 'Nostalgia of Mud' collection. Originally designed for women, men such as Steve Strange began wearing them on the London club scene in the early 1980s (below left). Many versions had an integral hood, a design feature that references the Roman practice of drawing the toga over the head when engaged in a sacrifice or other religious rite. Since the launch of her menswear label 'Man' in 1996, toga dresses have featured regularly in Westwood's collections. For her Spring/Summer 1997 collection, for instance, she produced a range of mini toga dresses in a length which would almost certainly have proved too dissolute for the average Roman citizen (below right).

left: Steve Strange in a toga dress by Vivienne Westwood, 'Nostalgia of Mud' collection, Autumn/Winter 1982–3
Photograph by Robyn Beech
Courtesy of Vivienne Westwood

right: Vivienne Westwood, Spring/Summer 1997
Photograph courtesy of Vivienne Westwood

MILITARY DRESS

Although the Romans disapproved of scanty clothing in the forum, they
actively promoted its use in military life. Most of our evidence for Roman
military costume comes from surviving portrait statues, many of which date
to the Empire and depict a triumphant general dressed in full ceremonial
armour (below right). Erected throughout the Roman world, they functioned
as an important form of honorific dedication.[16]

As Richard Gergel explains in 'Costume as Geographic Indicator:
Barbarians and Prisoners on Cuirassed Statue Breastplates' (2001),
two styles of armour prevailed in the Roman Empire: the so-called Classical
and Hellenistic cuirasses. Based on Greek prototypes, both have curved
lower edges and modelled surfaces which imitate the musculature of the
human torso. The difference lies in the type of skirt-like tabs or straps
attached to the cuirass. In the Classical model, one or more rows of round
or tongue-shaped hinged tabs or *pteryges* are fastened to the lower
edge of the cuirass. These hang over the single row of long leather straps
attached to the lower edge of the underlying vest. This row (or rows)
of tabs or *pteryges* are absent in the Hellenistic model. In its place is a
row of short leather straps which, in turn, hang over the single row
of long leather straps attached to the lower edge of the underlying vest.

Typically, the row of leather straps attached to the underlying
vest fell to mid-thigh, revealing the lower edge of the tunic beneath.
The usual length of the tunic was just above the knee, a length that not
only enhanced mobility, but also allowed the wearer to show off his legs
to best advantage. Indeed, the military garb of the Romans (and the
Greeks and Etruscans before them) did much to promote the leg as one
of the principal sites for the display of a man's strength, athleticism
and even sexual prowess. Skirts, and particularly those that revealed a

The Mars of Todi
Bronze, Etruscan, early 4th century
Vatican Museum
Courtesy of Flammarion/Art Resource, NY

large proportion of the male leg such as the Roman military tunic, allowed their wearers, specifically their youthful wearers, to flaunt their virility and masculinity. Even with the adoption of breeches and, later, trousers, the male leg continued to be one of the major sites for the display of a man's sexual and physical prowess.

John Galliano for Christian Dior brought a Roman military portrait statue to life for his Autumn/Winter 2000-2001 collection (page 43). Shown on the catwalk on a modern-day Mars, the god of war, Galliano's cuirass was as boldly ostentatious as any Roman example. Its defined musculature both aped and announced the model's hard, well-toned body. The single row of straps (made from the same material as the ornate bands decorating the cuirass) barely covered the model's hips and, since Galliano had not equipped him with a knee-length tunic, his modesty. With his well-developed legs proudly asserting his youth, strength and virile athleticism, the model's uncanny resemblance to the large 4th-century BCE Etruscan bronze statue of the *Mars of Todi* (above) would certainly not have been lost on Galliano.

above: **Christian Dior Haute Couture by John Galliano, Autumn/Winter 2000–2001**
Photograph courtesy of Maria Valentino/ MCV Photo

right: **Saint Dunstan, 12th-century copy of a 9th-century commentary on the Rule of Saint Benedict**
Courtesy of British Library, London

ECCLESIASTICAL DRESS

Although many of the garments that became the traditional liturgical or ceremonial vestments of Roman Catholic priests have their origins in Roman dress, they became distinctive sacred and religious dress during the Early Middle Ages. One of the original and primary functions of ecclesiastical dress, like Roman military dress, was to establish a symbolic space or distance between its wearer and the rest of society. Unlike Roman military dress, however, ecclesiastical dress was designed to deny and deflect the wearer's physical and sexual presence by the concealment of the body. The long, voluminous tunics worn by the clergy, like those worn by older and wealthier men in the Early Middle Ages, were designed to convey the wearer's dignity, modesty and respectability.

Prior to the fourth century, there was little difference between the clothes worn by priests and those worn by the laity. Indeed, during the Nerovian persecution of Christians in the first century, distinctive clothes would have been positively dangerous. However, it is particularly from the sixth century onwards that a certain number of secular garments took on a religious and symbolic character.[17] As Janet Mayo explains in *A History of Ecclesiastical Dress* (1984), 'By the end of the fifth century under the influence of the Byzantine spirit of minute classification, which prescribed a uniform for almost all classes of the Empire, clerical dress became distinctly and permanently fixed in its chief lines, marking the distinctions between the different orders of the clergy as well as between clergy and people.'[18]

An image of Saint Dunstan shows the style and arrangement of a priest's liturgical costume in its final stages of evolution (above). Beginning with the innermost vestment, he wears the white, floor-length *alb* with long narrow sleeves. Around his neck is the *amice*, a strip of stiff linen that creates a collar-like appearance. Over his *alb*, he wears the wide-sleeved *dalmatic*, which is decorated by an embroidered band at the hem. The characteristic side-split is just visible at the bottom right of the garment. His outermost vestment, the *chasuble*, is loose and flowing with a small, all-over pattern and an embroidered band around the edge. Over this is worn the *pallium*, a narrow band which encircles the upper arm and hangs down pendant from the centre front. Small crosses are interspersed with another cruciform pattern. His mitre, with broad orphrey, has two lappets or *infulae*, which end in fringes.[19]

John Galliano for Christian Dior presented an elaborate and fantastical interpretation of liturgical dress for his Autumn/Winter 2000-2001 collection (above). While bearing little resemblance

to traditional liturgical or ceremonial vestments, Galliano perfectly captured the elements of spectacle and solemnity required of such clothing. Made entirely from gold fabric, Galliano's exquisite robe or tunic recalls a story narrated by Theodoret, who became Bishop of Syria in 420. It is an account of the charge preferred against Cyril, Bishop of Jerusalem, before the Emperor Constantius: 'The Emperor Constantine, of famous memory, as a mark of honour to the Church of Jerusalem, had sent to Macarius, then bishop of that city, a sacred robe, made of threads of gold, which he should put upon him when performing the office of Holy Baptism. This robe, Acacius declared, had been sold by Cyril, and that a stage dancer had bought it and put it on, but that, in dancing, he fell and received injuries which proved fatal.'[20] Galliano's gold ensemble also references the liturgical vestments of the Late Middle Ages, which were richly decorated with the English medieval-style of embroidery known as *Opus Anglicanum*.

In terms of cut, Galliano's tunic bears a loose resemblance to the cassock or *soutane* worn by Roman Catholic priests. Unlike many liturgical vestments, the *soutane* did not develop from Roman secular dress but was adopted from Barbarian dress. The Council of Braga ordered its use in the late sixth century and, since then, it has been continually worn by the clergy up to today. Characteristically an ankle-length, long-sleeved tunic buttoning from the neck to the feet, the *soutane* is not reserved exclusively for the clergy and may be worn by servers, vergers and choristers. While universally worn by clergy as an undergarment in liturgical ceremonies, it can also be worn as an overgarment for indoor and outdoor wear. The *soutane* with a small cape and oversleeves is called the *zimara* (opposite).

In addition to Galliano, several other designers have also produced fashionable versions of the *soutane*. Jean Paul Gaultier created a wool version for his Autumn/Winter 1994–5 collection, while Donna Karan produced a version in black velvet for her Autumn/Winter 1997-8 collection. (below left). Less fanciful than Galliano's *soutane*, both Karan and Gaultier's versions reflect the *soutane's* original purpose, to declare the wearer's piety, dignity and humility. Black is the colour usually reserved for the clergy (white being reserved for the pope, red for cardinals and purple for bishops). Alexander McQueen for his Autumn/Winter 1998-9 collection also produced a version in black leather (below right). Sleeveless and paired with a red shirt, its length recalls a shorter style of *soutane* that emerged in the eighteenth century for horse-riding bishops, deans and archdeacons. Together with matching gaiters, this style forms an outfit still worn by some dignitaries today. McQueen's version also recalls the clerical coat or frock coat, the regular wear of the nineteenth-century clergyman. Like McQueen's version, this skirted clerical coat, which was retained by the clergy until the beginning of the twentieth century, was usually worn with trousers.

opposite: **Cardinal James Gibbons (1834–1921)**
Courtesy of Heritage Photographs ©1999

right: **Jean Paul Gaultier,**
Autumn/Winter 1994–5
Photograph courtesy of Maria Valentino/MCV Photo

far right: **Alexander McQueen, Autumn/Winter 1998–9**
Photograph courtesy of Maria Valentino/MCV Photo

GOWNS

Ecclesiastical dress, particularly liturgical or ceremonial dress, is characterized by layering. This strategy, which served to conceal and camouflage the natural contours of the body, had its origins in the Roman custom of wearing an inner tunic and an outer tunic. Among the upper classes, this practice continued throughout the Early Middle Ages. In the thirteenth century, the inner tunic came to be known as the *cote* and the outer tunic as the *surcote*. As worn by the privileged, the *cote* was ankle-length with long, tight-fitting sleeves. It differed markedly from tunics worn by men in earlier periods in that its bodice or upper section was fitted to the figure, an effect achieved by lacing the tunic at the side. Advances in tailoring techniques, such as the use of gores, inserts, lacing and pinning, occurred in the mid-twelfth century and resulted in a new, etiolated and elongated style of dress for men. This new emphasis on the male figure attracted the wrath of moralists who felt that the new, body-conscious style was both immodest and indecorous (particularly since the lacing often revealed the linen chemise or

undershirt beneath). *Surcotes* were made in a variety of different styles, including a sleeveless version with a round or horizontal neckline and wide armholes. The open *surcote* had very wide sleeves that revealed the *cote* underneath and, sometimes, even more of the lacing, causing further criticism from Medieval moralists.

Compared to men's fashions of the fourteenth century, those of the thirteenth century were positively timorous. From the end of the 1320s, cloth was cut to make garments fit like an outer skin, and, for many dress historians, fashion as we know it today was born.[21] Fashionable men discarded the long *cote* in favour of a short, tight tunic that revealed the shape of the body and proudly exposed the legs to public view. Like the short tunics worn by Roman soldiers (and, indeed, by labourers throughout the Middle Ages), the leg became the vehicle by which men could display their physical and sexual prowess. Churchmen and moralists viewed the new style with open hostility. Because of the possible exposure of the genitals, they denounced it as dissolute and foolhardy. Contemporary writers went so far

as to attribute the French defeat at the battle of Crecy in 1346 to a divine punishment for their pride in wearing such short, indecent clothes.[22] By the 1360s, the tunic had become so short that Pope Urban V attempted, unsuccessfully, to proscribe its use.[23]

Towards the end of the fourteenth century, as the tunic was reaching its limits of brevity, the *houppelande* made its appearance in Britain. The *houppelande* was called a 'gown' and its distinctive features were a loose fit, long, large sleeves and, later, a high collar.[24] The gown was pleated or gathered across the chest and belted high over the waist. Put on over the head, styles were either short, to the thighs, or long, for ceremonial occasions (above). A mid-calf length version, known as the *houppelande à mi-jamb* appeared in the 1400s. Again, the short versions received criticisms from moralists for their profligacy and wantonness. Long versions were denounced for their excessive and extravagant use of material. Even the dagged or cutwork decoration at the collar and edges of the gown was condemned on the grounds that it was a sign of pride or vanity.

opposite: **The monk Philippe de Maizieres presenting a book to Richard II, 1395–6**
Courtesy of British Library, London

above: **Vivienne Westwood, Autumn/Winter 1996–7**
Courtesy of Inez van Lamsweerde/Vinoodh Matadin/Art+Commerce Anthology

The *houppelande* had originated in France in the mid-fourteenth century and was initially worn as a housecoat over the *pourpoint*. Known in Britain as the doublet, the *pourpoint* was a short, padded, waist-length jacket with tight sleeves and a low, round neckline. Fastening down the front, the *pourpoint* closed with either laces or closely placed buttons. Strings sewn to the underside allowed for the attachment of hose which, at this period, were parti-coloured.

When worn under a short *houppelande*, the *pourpoint* inflated the chest, minimized the waist and, most importantly, exaggerated the length of the leg.

For her Autumn/Winter 1996–7 collection, Vivienne Westwood conflated the doublet or *pourpoint* and the *houppelande* to create a garment that she called a 'Host's Gown'. No longer two separate garments, the *pourpoint* formed the bodice or upper section of the floor-length *houppelande*.

In one version, which was produced in hot pink, the doublet fastened down the front and the lower half of the arms with ties or ribbons (overleaf). Another version had no fastenings, but was belted or girdled at the waist with a 'chatelaine', a chain created in the seventeenth century to carry watches and seals (above). Westwood chose a more up-to-date equipage, including gambling chips, a die, a whistle and a signature gold penis.

DIVIDED SKIRTS

From the late fifteenth century, it became possible to wear the tight-fitting doublet or *pourpoint* without a gown or over-garment. The leg, again, became the main vehicle for the projection of one's masculinity with its attendant associations of virility, strength and athleticism. At the same time, leg coverings assumed a new importance. With the evolution of tailoring techniques in the mid-fourteenth century and the advancement of fitted or shaped garments, the distinction between male and female clothing became more apparent. At its most basic, this distinction, which became more ingrained in subsequent centuries, manifested itself as bifurcated garments for men and non-bifurcated garments for women.

The Renaissance development of hose, however, meant that men often continued to wear skirted garments in conjunction with bifurcated garments. Originally made with separate legs, hose, by the fifteenth century, had developed into a garment similar to modern tights or stockings.[25] In the early sixteenth century, breeches were introduced and remained the standard male lower-body garment until the late eighteenth and early nineteenth centuries when trousers became fashionable. A portrait of Henry VIII dating to 1536 depicts the monarch sporting both hose and breeches. Worn, as they are, under a short, loose gown and full-skirted tunic or jerkin, they are barely visible and almost relegated to the status of underwear, or rather, undergarments (overleaf). A similar effect is achieved by Walter van Beirendonck, who showed a layered, transparent skirt over a pair of breeches for his Aestheticterrorists Spring/Summer 2003 collection (right). Although his source of inspiration is clearly the dress of the *Incroyables*, the giddy young men of 1790s France, by giving prominence to the skirt, the breeches become impotent and emasculated.

opposite: **Vivienne Westwood, Autumn/Winter 1996–7**
Photograph by Marco Lanza for *Harper's Bazaar
Italio Uomo*, 1996
Styled by Ruben Modigliani
Courtesy of Marco Lanza

right: **Aestheticterrorists by Walter van Beirendonck,
'Respect, Rethink, React' collection,
Spring/Summer 2003**
Photograph by Donald Graham for *Paper Magazine*, 2003
Styled by Timothy Reukauffor
Courtesy of Donald Graham/Helen Roche

left: **Anon, Portrait of Henry VIII after Hans Holbein's mural at Whitehall**
Oil on panel, late 1536
Courtesy of Walker Art Gallery, Liverpool

right: **Anon, Robert Dudley, Earl of Leicester**
Oil on panel, c.1575–80
Courtesy of National Portrait Gallery, London

In the sixteenth and seventeenth centuries, certain types or styles of breeches gave the illusion of actual skirted garments. Trunk hose, for instance, which made their appearance in the mid-sixteenth century, covered the upper part of the thigh with balloon-like magnitude (above right). Moralists attacked the stuffed (bomasted) trunk hose on the grounds of effeminacy, arguing that they echoed the curves of female hips. Indeed, by the early 1560s, trunk hose were so large and globe-like that proclamations were passed to reduce their size.[26] In 1562, specific instructions were issued to tailors to limit the amount of lining and stuffing in hose, to prevent the 'monstrous and outrageous greatness of hosen'.[27] Tailors were urged to make them of modest proportions, not 'to be bolstered, but to lye juste unto their legges, as in ancient tyme was accustomed.'[28] The shortening of trunk hose in the 1580s provoked further criticism from moralists who argued that they allowed the wearer's legs to be seen almost as though naked. Montaigne described them as 'filthy breeches, that so openly shew our secret parts'.[29]

left: Gerard Ter Borch, *Man in Black*, c.1673
The Louvre, Paris ©RMN/Art Resource, New York

right: William Larkin, Richard Sackville,
3rd Earl of Dorset, 1613
Courtesy of Ranger's House (English Heritage),
The Suffolk Collection

Slop breeches became fashionable in the early seventeenth century. Padded, pleated and usually gathered under the knee, they also gave the appearance of a skirt (above right). Even more voluminous were the 'rhinegraves' or 'petticoat breeches' introduced in the late 1650s, although they did not become universal until the early 1660s (above left). Primarily a court fashion, petticoat breeches were cut so full that Samuel Pepys commented in his diary, 'Among other things, I met with Mr Townsend, who told of his mistake the other day, to put both legs through one of his knees, and went so all day.'[30] The diarist John Evelyn disliked petticoat breeches as he thought they were effeminate and turned men into a 'kind of Hermaphrodite'.[31] Indeed, the Oxford antiquary Anthony Wood writing in 1663 found it 'a strange effeminate age when men strive to imitate women in their apparel, viz long periwigs, patches in their faces, painting, short wide breeches like petticoats, muffs, and their clothes highly scented, bedecked with ribbons of all colours.'[32]

Despite the fact that trunk hose, slops and petticoat breeches were all bifurcated, they presented the viewer with a unified, skirt-like

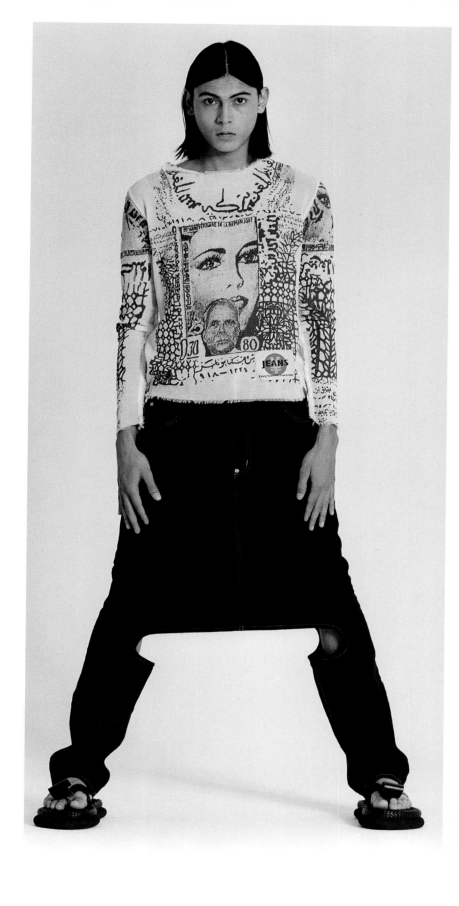

left: **Yohji Yamamoto, Spring/Summer 1988**
Photograph by Nick Knight for *Arena,* 1988
Styled by Marc Ascoli
Courtesy of Nick Knight

right: **Michiko Koshino, Spring/Summer 1999**
Photograph by Francesco Valentino
Courtesy of Michiko Koshino

front. Following in the footsteps of Jacobean gallants, various twentieth-century youth cultures have exploited the allure of voluminous trousers from Oxford bags and zoot suits to flares and baggy jeans. Several designers have played with the tension between skirts and trousers, often creating hybrid garments that are bifurcated, but give the illusion of being non-bifurcated. Like Esterel and Gaultier, both Yohji Yamamoto and Comme des Garçons have created garments with wrap-around aprons (opposite). Reminiscent of the baggy jeans worn by skaters and promoted by hip-hop, Michiko Koshino has created a hybrid garment that conflates jeans with a knee-length denim skirt (above). The British designer Tony Phillips has also looked to hip hop for a range of skirts designed with a snap that gives the wearer the choice to wear it as a skirt or trousers (overleaf).

left: **Tony Phillips, 1996**
Photograph by Jeremy Murch for *i-D*, 1996
Courtesy of Jeremy Murch

right: **Bernard Lens III, A group of men
and women in a landscape, 1725**
Courtesy of the Witt Collection,
Courtauld Institute of Art, London

COATS

Throughout the 1660s, coats of various types were worn with the doublet and petticoat breeches. By 1670, however, the capacious petticoat breeches proved unwieldy and were deemed unsightly. They were discarded in favour of narrower breeches, closed at the knee, which presented more balanced and harmonious proportions. At the same time, the doublet was replaced with a vest or waistcoat. This ensemble of coat, vest and breeches became the forerunner of the modern three-piece suit.

In its early form, the coat was roughly tubular in shape. By the 1690s, however, it began to look and behave somewhat like a skirt or dress form. While the upper portion became increasingly fitted to the body, the lower portion, called 'skirts', became progressively wider. Stiffened with buckram or horse-hair, the coat's skirts fanned out over the hips, a silhouette which matched the bell-shaped skirts of women's dresses.[33] By the early eighteenth century, the skirts had become so generous that a woman in *The Spectator* observed, 'The skirt of your fashionable coats

forms as large a circumference as our petticoats.'[34] A drawing of 1725 by Bernard Lens reveals the feminine silhouette achieved by such full-skirted coats (above). Depicting men and women promenading in a public park, the men's coats, which fall to the knees, almost conceal the breeches, a feature that serves to enhance their skirt- or dress-like appearance.

This feminine or, rather, androgynous silhouette was highly desirable for much of the eighteenth century. The dress coat's inherent elegance has guaranteed its self-conscious repetition in the

twentieth century. Alexander McQueen, for instance, created a version
that recalled the swaggering cut of the period. McQueen designed
the coat in collaboration with David Bowie who wore it on the album cover
of *Earthling* (left). As Bowie comments, 'I wanted to recontextualize
Pete Townshend's jacket of the Sixties, but then I got a bit carried away
and thought it would look rather nice as a frock coat. Then Alex got
even further carried away and cut bits of it up.'[35] Ruined yet precisely cut,
Bowie and McQueen's coat captures perfectly the satirical charge of
Hogarth's *Rake's Progress* (1735).

In terms of cut, Bowie and McQueen's design recalls the dress coats
of the early eighteenth century. As Bowie's comments indicate, it was
also conceptualized as a frock coat. Made in plain, practical materials, the
frock coat (initially referred to as the 'frock') appeared in fashionable
circles as informal wear in the 1730s. A loose-fitting coat, it was originally
worn by working men, but was taken up by gentlemen for greater comfort
and ease of movement. By the end of the eighteenth century, the frock
coat had begun to take on a definite national character. In a passage in the
Gray's-Inn Journal, the writer, while preparing for a trip to Paris, writes:

'*Our next Care was to equip ourselves in the Fashion of the Country.
Accordingly we sent for a Taylor, and Jack Commons, who jabbers a little
French, directed him to make us two Suits; which he brought us the next
Morning at Ten o'Clock, and made complete Frenchmen of us. But for my
part, Harry, I was so damned uneasy in a full-dressed Coat, with hellish long
Skirts, which I had never been used to, that I thought myself as much
deprived of my Liberty, as if I had been in the Bastile; and I frequently sighed
for my little loose Frock, which I look upon as an Emblem of our happy
Constitution; for it lays a Man under no easy Restraint, but leaves it in his
Power to do as he pleases.*'[36]

In the nineteenth century the frock coat became one of the definitive symbols
of British masculinity and even empire. While simpler and less structured
than the eighteenth-century dress coat, the frock, too, developed into a
full-skirted coat that aped the ideal female silhouette. As can be seen from
the sketch *The Round Pond* (1832), the skirt- or dress-like appearance
of the frock coat was enhanced by skin-tight pantaloons, which traced the
natural shape of the leg and suggested an air of nudity (above).

Although the frock coat's popularity waned after the First World War,
it was later appropriated by various subcultural groups like Goths and
New Romantics as part of a historicist wardrobe. At the same time,
various designers have recapitulated its breathtaking tailoring. For his
Autumn/Winter 1999-2000 collection, Masaki Matsushima created a version
that conflated the frock coat with the longer 'great coat' popular during
the first half of the nineteenth century (overleaf). Cut close to the torso,
the skirts flare out from the waist in a cascade of box pleats. John Bartlett
produced a version with skirts that recall the fulsome Scottish kilt for
his Autumn/Winter 2000-2001 collection (page 61). Cut away at the front,
Bartlett's frock coat resembled the riding coat adopted as informal wear in
the late eighteenth century.

left: **Coat by Masaki Matsushima,**
Autumn/Winter 1999–2000
Photograph by Lee Jenkins for *The Face*, 1999
Styled by Allan Kennedy
Courtesy of Lee Jenkins/CLM London

above: **Coat by John Bartlett, Autumn/Winter 1997–8**
Photograph by Ram Shergill for *Attitude*, 2000
Styled by Neil Berryman
Courtesy of Ram Shergill

BOYS IN DRESSES

To the far left of *The Round Pond* are two boys wearing dresses. From the sixteenth century, boys wore long robes or dresses during the first few years of infancy. When they reached a suitable age, anywhere between two and eight, they gave up their dresses and started wearing breeches or trousers. This event was marked by a 'breeching ceremony'. It was an important occasion in any household, as is evident by a description given by one member of an aristocratic family in the seventeenth century:

'You cannot believe the great concerne that was in the whole family here last Wednesday, it being the day that the taylor was to help dress little Frank in his breeches in order to the making an everyday suit by it. Never had any bride that was to be drest upon her wedding night more hands about her, some the legs, and some the arms, the taylor butt'ning, and others putting on the sword, and so many lookers on that had I not a finger amongst them I could not have seen him. When he was quite dreste, he acted his part as any of them... They are very fit, everything, and he looks taller and prettyer than his coats [petticoats].'[37]

Several theories have been put forward to explain boys in dresses. One theory suggests that because of the high mortality rate among infants in the eighteenth and nineteenth centuries, parents were reluctant to become too attached

left: **Anon, Portrait of Alfred Fuller, aged four, 1870**
The Victoria and Albert Museum

right: **John Galliano, Autumn/Winter 2000–2001**
Photograph courtesy of Maria Valentino/MCV Photo

opposite: **Walter van Beirendonck, 'Futureday' collection,**
Spring/Summer 2004
Courtesy of Walter van Beirendonck

or identify a particular child as an heir during infancy. Another theory claims that it was a practical measure for dealing with childhood incontinence, while a third asserts that by the age of six or seven a male child was probably capable of putting on his own breeches. In the latter half of the nineteenth century, it was thought that if you distinguished between the sexes at too early an age, it might provoke precocious sexual curiosity.

Although garments for boys and girls are linguistically indistinguishable, portraits of children from the eighteenth and nineteenth centuries use various strategies to distinguish the gender of their sitters.[38] Most frequently, male children are depicted with stereotypically masculine props, alluding to future careers or innate masculine virtues. These included drums or trumpets, hobby-horses or crops, faithful dogs or wooden swords (above). Where boys and girls are represented together, the boy's dress may be distinguished from the girl's by means of colour, cut or accessories like plumed hats. To the modern eye, these differences are fairly subtle, but they were more legible to a contemporary audience.

Designers have drawn on the image of boys in dresses as a figure of gamin nostalgia in their catwalk presentations of men in dresses. Just as boys were depicted in paintings with stereotypically masculine props, designers often style their models with manly accessories to negate the perceived femininity of their dresses. John Galliano for his Autumn/Winter

2000–2001 collection showed a chiffon dress paired with a waistcoat and heavy wellington boots (above). With a saucepan as a hat and a painted, play-time, beard and moustache, Galliano's man in a dress is imbued with a Pierrot-esque theatricality. Walter van Beirendonck showed a more subversive interpretation of men in dresses for his Spring/Summer 2004 collection (right). He put adolescent boys in transparent dresses paired with bowler hats that evoked the violent naïveté of *A Clockwork Orange*. By contrast, Jean Paul Gaultier, who showed men in elegant fifties-style ball gowns for his Autumn/Winter 1996–7 collection, brought to mind the *joie de vivre* of a small boy dressing up in his mother's Diors or Balenciagas.

EXOTICISM

As anthropological accounts of dress reveal, there is
no natural link between an item of clothing and
femininity and masculinity, but instead an arbitrary
set of associations that are culturally specific.[1]
It is the context in which articles of clothing are worn
that determines whether they are masculine or
feminine. Designers of the skirt for men have often
looked to non-Western cultures for sources of
both inspiration and legitimization. They have seized
on particular garment types like the sarong,
caftan, *kurta* or *qamis* and kimono. In terms of both
design and styling, the results are often highly
exoticized versions of these 'culturally authentic'
garments. Exoticism involves a dual process of
nostalgia and alienation, a longing for a place that
one has never been, or a culture that exists only
in the Western imagination. Non-Western cultures are
often perceived as static and timeless – a utopian,
genderless paradise. But, as in the West, clothing is
not only dynamic in most non-Western cultures,
but serves to mark a definite distinction between the
sexes. However, it is the exotic, even romantic
connotations of non-Western skirted garments that
have proved most attractive to both designers
and fashion-conscious men.

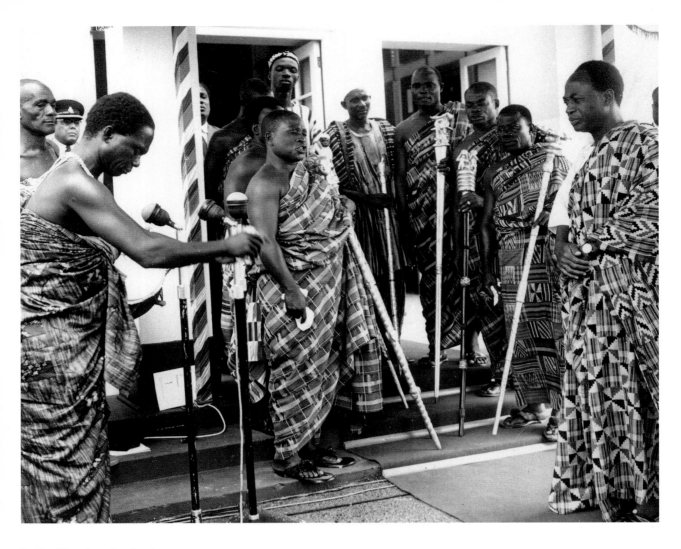

President Nkrumah at a State Opening
of Parliament, Accra, Ghana, c.1975
Courtesy of Associated Press

UNCUT CLOTH

Climate plays a critical role in the
clothing traditions of many
non-Western cultures. In areas
where arid, tropical or sub-tropical
conditions prevail, the traditional
clothes worn by both men
and women, like those worn by
men and women in many
civilizations of the Ancient World,
are usually comprised of a length
of uncut rectangular fabric draped
and wrapped around the body.
Since little clothing is needed in
such hot and humid environments,
draped costume is a practical
necessity. In pre-industrial and
subsistence societies, it is also an
economic necessity as draped
costume allows for the wearing of
lengths of cloth as they come

off the loom. In societies that rely
on uncut cloth, the significant
site of meaning becomes the textile
itself. Its colour, pattern and texture
reflect regional and gendered
identities, as well as the age, rank
and status of the wearer.

BODYWRAPS

There are numerous ways in which
a length of uncut, rectangular fabric
can be disposed on the body.
Throughout West Africa, a common
style, worn particularly by adult
men, involves draping the length
of cloth on the body in a style
reminiscent of the Roman toga.
This is the traditional style worn by
adult men among the Asante of
Ghana (above). A long, rectangular
piece of cloth is wrapped around

the body, passed over the left
shoulder and brought around the
body once more before being
secured. Normally, the left shoulder
and upper arm are kept covered
by the cloth, restricting the
wearer's movement. As Malcolm
McLeod observes in *The Asante*
(1981), 'The left hand is considered
inauspicious and dirty in some
contexts (it is used in wiping
excrement from the body and in
certain reversed, "bad" rituals), and
covering of the left shoulder and
upper arm befits the status of that
part of the body.'[2] Pulling the cloth
off the shoulder and rolling it
into a thick girdle above the waist
exposes the torso. This style is
worn to show respect before senior
people or when approaching

left: Emporio Armani, Spring/Summer 1999
Photograph courtesy of Niall McInerney

right: Maasai warrior, Kenya, 1991
Photograph courtesy of Peter Lavery

ancestral stools. It is also worn when vigorous exertion is planned.

These large cloths are made from a variety of fabrics, such as *adinkra*. Traditionally, *adinkra* cloths are dark red, blue, green or brown decorated with designs in black dye. Originally, strip cloth was used, but today imported cotton broadcloth is the more common material.[3] Abstract designs are stamped on the cloth with small calabash stamps dipped in a tar-like substance called *adinkra aduro*. Similar designs can also be found in the low relief decorations of traditional houses. Darker cloths are worn to express grief and mourning while lighter shades are now worn as a sort of 'Sunday best'. The most striking of all cloths, however, is *kente*. It is made from locally woven narrow strips of cloth sewn together to make up a wider piece of cloth with complex and dazzling patterns. Most *kente* cloths are named according to their warp pattern, although some are named after people (usually rulers), trees, plants, birds and animals. *Kente* was made famous by the late President Nkrumah of Ghana, who was much given to being photographed wearing the traditional Asante cloth. Indeed, as Venice Lamb comments in *West African Weaving* (1975), 'Under the influence of the late President of Ghana, Kwame Nkrumah, *kente* became something more than purely Ghanaian and almost the uniform of pan-Africanism.'[4]

The draping of a rectangular length of fabric on the body can also be seen among various nomadic tribes in East Africa, such as the semi-nomadic Maasai. A pastoral people, the Maasai live in Kenya and Tanzania, in the Great Rift Valley. In the Western imagination, the Maasai's fierce, warlike image was channelled through various travelogues written by European explorers in the late nineteenth century, perhaps most notably Joseph Thompson's *Masai Land* (1885). Traditionally, all young warriors wear a length of cotton broadcloth wrapped around the body and tied over one shoulder (above).[5] Known as *shuka*, it was originally dyed with red ochre, although today many Maasai wear colourful factory-made versions. Styles or, rather, lengths, differ from region to region. Ilkisongo warriors of Tanzania, for instance, wear them below the knee, while Ilpurko warriors from Kenya prefer short versions to expose their thighs. The Ilkisongo are often criticized by the Ilpurko for the impracticality of their costume, just as the Ilpurko are often criticized by the Ilkisongo for the indecency of theirs.[6]

The clothing of the Maasai has inspired several contemporary designers. Giorgio Armani, for instance, designed various versions of the *shuka* for his Spring/Summer 1999 collection (page 67). In one version, Armani lightly wrapped a rectangular length of fabric around the model's body and tied it over his right shoulder. Underneath, the model wore a pair of swimming trunks, into which one of the bottom corners of the length of fabric was tucked, revealing his muscular thigh as he walked down the runway. References to the Maasai's war-like reputation could be seen in the model's short, cropped hair and his tough, thick-soled shoes. These details not only enhanced the aggressive masculinity of the ensemble but, combined with a hooded top, imbued the outfit with an air of contemporaneity.

below: **Labourers in Oelolk, Timor, Indonesia, late 20th Century**
Photograph courtesy of Mattiebelle Gittinger, Washington DC

right: **Group of men and boys, Thailand, late 19th century**
Photograph ©Hulton-Deutsch Collection/CORBIS

WAISTCLOTHS

Another way of wearing a length of uncut, rectangular fabric is to simply wrap it around the hips or waist. This style can be found in most cultures with a tradition of draped costume, including many areas of Asia, Africa, Oceania and the Americas. However, it is perhaps most closely associated with South and Southeast Asia. Along with the kilt, the waistcloth, which in the West has become widely known by the term 'sarong', is the most popular and re-visited skirt form promoted by stylists, designers and photographers. It is also one of the more acceptable and, in certain contexts, most widely worn skirt forms among fashionable men, largely due to its practicality and perceived 'genderless' status. In the cultures where the waistcloth is indigenous, however, distinctions between those of men and women are immediately recognizable to the local population.

Throughout Indonesia, both men and women wear a variety of waistcloths. In Java, for instance, both sexes traditionally wear a rectangular textile, typically decorated with batik designs. When worn by men it is called *bebed* and when worn by women it is known as *tapih*. While both men

Man, Chaibasa, Jharkhand, India, 2000
Photograph courtesy of Marcus Leatherdale

opposite: **Houseboy, Banaras, India, 1999**
Photograph courtesy of Marcus Leatherdale

and women wear the waistcloth wrapped around the hips, they use different methods of securing the fabric in place. Men use a belt or a knot and women use a stiff fabric band called a *stagen*.[7] Similarly, in Timor, men wear a large rectangular length of cotton comprising two or three woven panels sewn together. It is wrapped about the hips and knotted at the waist (page 68). A similar length of cloth is worn over the shoulders to protect against the morning and evening chill (during the heat of the day, it is knotted around the waist, over the first cloth). As Mattiebelle Gittinger observes in *Splendid Symbols: Textiles and Tradition in Indonesia* (1979), 'Etiquette demands that a man of lesser rank who is wearing his shoulder cloth immediately drop it to his waist when meeting a superior.'[8] Traditionally, these textiles are cinched into place by a long, narrow cloth belt with carefully wrought tapestry and twined designs at the ends. By contrast, the traditional costume worn by Timor women comprises a narrow tubular garment worn like a sheath.

Men and women in many areas of Thailand also wear waistcloths (page 69). Traditionally they are worn in two different styles. The first, known as the *pha chong kaben*, comprises a rectangular textile wrapped around the waist, passed between the legs and tucked in at the back to form loose pantaloon-style trousers. The second style comprises a rectangular cloth sewn with one

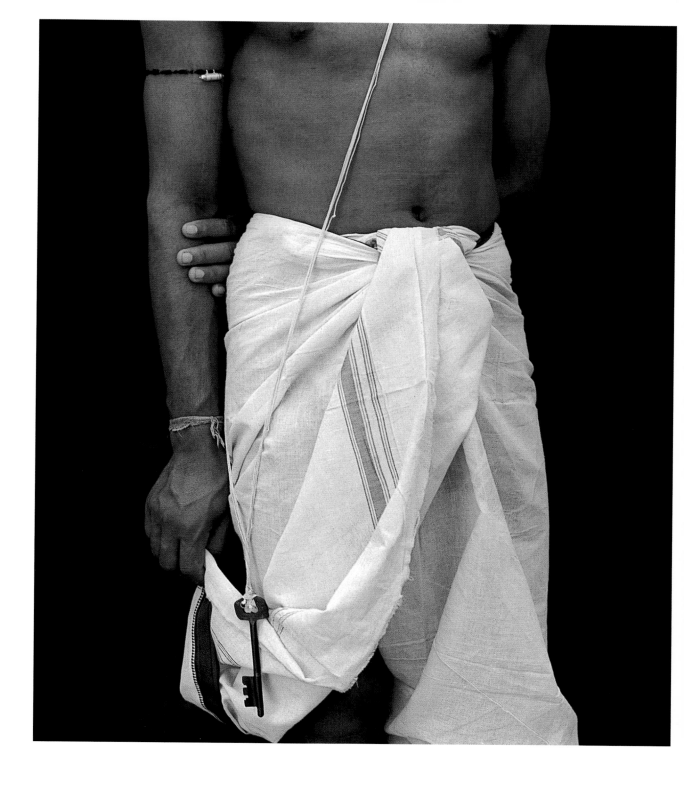

side seam to create a tubular garment tucked at the waist with a pleat or knot. Men's versions are called *pha sarongs*, while the version for women is known as *phasin* (and often reveals two side seams). Women's *phasins* tend to be worn longer, and vary more in terms of colour and pattern. By contrast men's *pha sarongs* tend to be restricted to plaids, stripes and plied yarn patterns. Traditionally, they were worn shorter to reveal a set of intricate tattoos, which usually extended from above the waist to just below the knee.

In India, waistcloths are more commonly associated with men's dress than women's dress. Indian men wear two styles of waistcloth, both of which are made from single lengths of uncut cloth. In India, unsewn cloth is considered holy or sacred (gifts consisting of lengths of cloth have deep-rooted resonance in many of India's Hindu and Muslim religious traditions).[9] The most common style is the *dhoti* (above left). Although worn in a number of ways, the most popular method involves wrapping the fabric around the midriff, pulling one end through the legs and tucking it at the back to resemble loose trousers, not unlike the Thai *pha chong kaben*. The *dhotis* worn by Hindus are usually white with distinctive narrow borders. The second style is the *lungi*, and is commonly worn in Pakistan, Bangladesh and parts of India (above). It differs from the *dhoti* in that it is simply wrapped around the waist.

Gender signifiers are often eschewed or overlooked in fashionable versions
of South and Southeast Asian waistcloths seen on the catwalk. For many
designers, the waistcloth becomes a vehicle for the promotion of unisex
dressing and the endorsement of an androgynous body. In a photograph by
Jean-Marie Périer for French *Elle*, a man and a woman wear identical
waistcloths from Jean Paul Gaultier's Autumn/Winter 1994–5 'The Big
Journey' collection (left). Both models are wearing the same style
of shoes and jacket with matching hairstyles. With bodies mirroring each
other and their faces turned to the camera, they are presented as Gaultier's
vision of the universality of clothing. In an earlier collection, Gaultier
presented the *dhoti* as an item for the unisex wardrobe (above). On the
catwalk, he dressed a man and woman in black *dhotis* with matching
jackets. Only the man's shaved head and the woman's coiffure remained
as signs of masculinity and femininity. Gaultier has also promoted
the sari, traditionally worn by women in India, in his menswear collections.
In his Spring/Summer 1997 collection he showed a range of sari-suits,
including a short version in a blue and white pinstripe.

Emporio Armani, Spring/Summer 1990
Photograph by Aldo Fallai
Courtesy of Armani Press, Milan

right: Emporio Armani, Spring/Summer 1998
Photograph by Aldo Fallai
Courtesy of Armani Press, Milan

Both designers and the men who wear them regard the waistcloth as an informal, leisured garment. Worn either at home or on the beach, the waistcloth represents escapism and relaxation. It announces 'I am off duty' (above). As Giorgio Armani comments, 'I have designed many sarongs as a way of introducing a new level of comfort and practicality into men's wardrobes. My feeling is that given the proper context, men experience no difficulty in wearing them. Most men probably feel more comfortable wearing a sarong in a relaxed vacation environment.'[10] As a site of fashionability, the beach has traditionally been a place less governed by conventional dress codes, freeing men to experiment with their self-image and self-presentation. No longer an unusual sight on the beach, the sarong has replaced the habit of wearing a towel wrapped around the waist.

Although waistcloths have been most successful as beachwear, several designers have attempted to promote them as formal wear and even as work wear, despite the fact that the office is usually perceived as a place in which dress codes are fixed and intransigent. Indeed, in 1995, a man lost his case against Hackney Council in London, which had banned him from wearing a skirt to work.[11] Designers such as Paul Smith,

Giorgio Armani and Roy Krejberg for Kenzo, however, have attempted
to bridge the gap between the waistcloth as beachwear and the waistcloth
as formal or work wear (page 75). Both Smith and Armani, for instance,
have styled their waistcloths with shirts (and in the case of Armani,
shirts and ties), while Krejberg has designed 'sarong suits' comprising
a sarong with a tailored jacket (below). Other designers like Philip Dubuc
and Jeff Griffin have tried to urbanize their sarongs to encourage men to
adopt them as fashionable street wear. As Dubuc explains, 'I have designed
a variety of "urban" sarongs with pockets in an attempt to make them
more practical, versatile and above all masculine. Men wear them in the
summer with a jacket as part of a suit, or more casually with a T-shirt
and trainers.'[12] Jeff Griffin combines his sarongs with hooded jackets and
sweatshirts to create a look 'relevant to the streets of London'.[13]
But even Griffin concedes that 'Men might wear sarongs to clubs, but
outside of this context, they would feel very uncomfortable. We are a long
way from men wearing sarongs as street wear.'[14] Paul Smith agrees,
although remains optimistic, 'At the moment, the acceptability of sarongs
for men is pretty much restricted to the beach. Outside of that context,
they are seen as something a fashion victim would wear. However,
this might change as the world becomes more multi-cultural and people
become more open-minded.'[15]

Men often wear waistcloths in order to project an image of
sensitivity and even vulnerability. In the John McTiernan's re-make of the
film *The Thomas Crown Affair* (1999), the icy, impenetrable Thomas
Crown, played by Pierce Brosnan, adopts a waistcloth in a scene in which
he reveals his more relaxed and unguarded nature. This image has
been promoted by several designers, including Donna Karan and Dolce and
Gabbana (below right). Both designers have shown waistcloths on the
catwalk with large, chunky sweaters and cardigans. Intended to convey the
qualities of warmth and strength, they are designed to show men as
comfortable with themselves. As Donna Karan comments, 'I prefer to use
the word "wrap" than "skirt". Wrap refers to the "function" rather than
the "gender" of the design. For me, it's a classic design, one that has been
worn by both men and women throughout history and across cultures.
It is a garment that enhances the wearer's feelings of comfort and freedom.
In my mind, a wrap looks best on a man who has a strong sense of "self"...
A man should wear a wrap, not the other way round.'[16]

far left: Kenzo by Roy Krejberg,
Autumn/Winter 2000–2001
Courtesy of XRX

left: Dolce & Gabbana, Spring/Summer 1994
Courtesy of Dolce & Gabbana

opposite: *Man in White/Woman in Black*,
Morocco 1974
Photograph ©Irving Penn
Courtesy of *Vogue*

ROBES

Many men prefer to wear 'authentic' waistcloths rather than 'designer' waistcloths, desiring to present an image of being well travelled, with its attendant associations of enlightened or conspicuous consumption. Perhaps the first garment to be marketed to men on this basis was the caftan, which not only acted as a form of travel snobbery when worn 'at home' in the West, but also self-consciously announced the wearer's liberalism, particularly in terms of his racial politics. When individuals wore the caftan as a symbol of their rejection of Western values and aspirations, it fell into the category of 'protest fashion'.

Turkish in origin, the caftan is worn by both men and women throughout North Africa. Traditionally, it has a narrow central section, folded double, with an open slit neck. Sleeve sections are added to the sides on a straight seam, and panels are inserted into the sides. The absence of curved cutting is compensated for by the use of underarm gussets. It is most usually worn loose down to the floor. The Moroccan caftan, or *qaftane*, usually fastens all the way down by a row of small buttons worked in thread. Women's *qaftanes* tend to be made from more luxurious fabrics, richly decorated with braids and edgings. Usually, an over-garment, known as the *farajiya*, is worn over the *qaftane*. Often made from a lighter, more transparent material, it is cut the same as the *qaftane*. These two robes are generally cinched in at the waist by a belt or *mdomma*. Traditionally, scholars and high-ranking officials wear the *qaftane* and *farajiya*. The most common article of dress among Moroccan men is the *jellaba (below)*.

The *jellaba* is a short-sleeved outer garment with a hood, slightly slit at front, back and sides. It is made from either imported or locally produced cloth, the weight of which varies according to the season. Colours and patterns also vary depending on trends and personal taste, although white always lends an aristocratic air to the wearer.[17]

Men throughout the Arab Peninsula wear caftans constructed along similar lines to those worn in North Africa. In Saudi Arabia, the caftan is referred to as the *thawb* (although it has also been called the *merodan*, *woniya* or *shillahat*). Usually, its neckline is high and round, generally with a banded collar or *aga* (above). The buttoned opening at centre front reaches to the middle chest. Variations include a Western shirt collar that is matched by shirtsleeve cuffs.[18] The *thawb* also has side pockets and, generally, another pocket on

the left breast. It is usually made from white or cream-coloured cotton and polyester. Often, a mantle known as a *bisht* or *mishlah* is worn over the *thawb*.

Caftans or caftan-like garments are found in most Islamic cultures throughout the world. The Hausa, a Muslim peoples now living in Niger and Northwest Nigeria, for instance, wear long, expansive caftan-like tunics, often embroidered on the chest opening, over loose trousers. Designed to cover the body, with the exception of the face, feet and hands, caftans almost certainly developed as a practical response to the arid conditions of most Muslim countries, providing both insulation and protection against the sun. However, these practical aspects have become Islamic custom. Total coverage of both the male and female form is a well-established Muslim tradition. As Jean

Besancenot explains in *Costumes of Morocco* (1990), 'the good Muslim should be ready at any moment for prayer, which is carried out so often during the course of the day, and hence wears clothes which modestly hide the form of the body while at the same time possessing the fullness required by the prostrate positions adopted.'[19]

Inspired by the 'otherness' of the exotic east, hippies during the late 1960s and early 1970s adopted caftans as a protest against middle-class capitalist values. As Rebecca Arnold points out in *Fashion, Desire and Anxiety: Image and Morality in the 20th Century* (2001), 'The hippie's loose, flowing garments were an emblem of inner freedom, and liberation from the rule-driven lifestyle of those caught in the treadmill of office jobs and "respectable" domestic life.'[20] Their natural, bohemian style showed contempt

for the mainstream and, in the United States, was a 'protest-fuelled
renunciation of the American dream and the ethics it stood for, in particular
the American government's policies concerning the Vietnam War.'[21] At the
same time, their caftans and long hair, sported by both men and women,
served to blur the visual distinctions between the sexes. In Britain, caftans
were imported from North Africa in vast numbers to fulfil the demand for
authenticity (top). Before long, however, designers such as Yves Saint
Laurent and Rudolph Moshammer began creating fashionable versions as
informal and semi-formal wear (above). As Paul Smith explains, caftans
even appeared on the highstreet: 'Granny Takes A Trip on the King's Road…
sold real kaftans, for instance, beautiful, hand-made garments from

Afghanistan with tiny mirrors. You couldn't get them anywhere else. But then Lord John would get hold of the look and suddenly you had kaftans everywhere, albeit horrible ones, and the look went mainstream on the high street.'[22]

Since the late 1960s, designers have continued to create fashionable re-interpretations of the caftan. Many, like Vivienne Westwood, have played with its formal elements, creating versions in hot pink and canary yellow (below left). Others, like Roberto Cavalli and Sean 'Puffy' Combs, have created versions with novel prints (below right). Like many designers who create skirts for men, one of Cavalli's motivations was to generate press interest. Unexpectedly, however, his caftans proved enormously successful in the market. As he comments, 'When I presented my collection I was not very concerned about the critics. I am, of course, aware of the fact that the more you surprise, the more you get in terms of press coverage. What I did not predict, however, was the buyers' feedback. The response was absolutely fabulous – the caftan was the best-selling item of my collection.'[23] The fact that Cavalli's caftans were cut closer to the body may have contributed to their success. It was a tactic used by Thierry Mugler in his Spring/Summer 2003 collection (bottom left). Unlike 'authentic' North

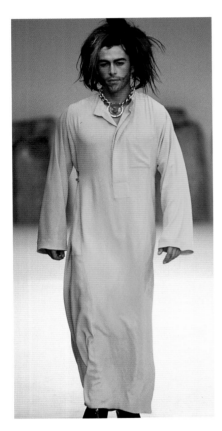

top left: **Vivienne Westwood, Autumn/Winter 1998–9**
Photograph courtesy of Niall McInerney

top right: **Roberto Cavalli, Spring/Summer 2002**
Photograph by Ugo Camera
Courtesy of Roberto Cavalli

bottom left: **Thierry Mugler, Spring/Summer 2003**
Photograph courtesy of Maria Valentino/MCV Photo

bottom right: **Jean Paul Gaultier, Spring/Summer 1996**
Courtesy of Jean Paul Gaultier.

opposite
above: **Miguel Adrover, Spring/Summer 2003**
Photograph courtesy of Maria Valentino/MCV Photo

below: **Moschino advertising campaign, Spring/Summer 1998**
Photograph by Michael Roberts/Maconochie
Courtesy of Moschino

far right: **Moschino by Rossella Jardini, Spring/Summer 2002**
Photograph courtesy of Christophe Kutner/
Michele Filomeno

African or Middle Eastern caftans, Mugler's versions were designed to reveal rather than conceal the body. Pushing the boundaries of decency or rather modesty even further, Jean Paul Gaultier created caftans in transparent fabrics, revealing even more of the male physique (page 80).

In the first half of the twentieth century, several Middle Eastern Heads of State, such as the Shah of Persia and King Farouk of Egypt, adopted Western-style clothing for formal occasions.[24] While today this trend has reversed, it inspired a trend among many Middle Eastern men of wearing their caftans with Western, tailored jackets. This trend, in turn, inspired the work of designers such as Miguel Adrover and Rossella Jardini for Moschino. For his Spring/Summer 2003 'Citizen of the World' collection, Adrover showed caftans worn with two-piece suits (below left). While these caftans were of his own design, Jardini for her Spring/Summer 2002 collection paired 'authentic' caftans with jackets and trousers (below). Earlier, Franco Moschino produced a denim caftan for his Spring/Summer 'Moschino jeans … whoever you are!' 1998 press campaign. For another press campaign, Moschino created a long, white shirt, paired with a tie and black trilby. It was a style that reflected the Saudi Arabian *thawb*, tailored with shirt collar and cuffs (bottom).

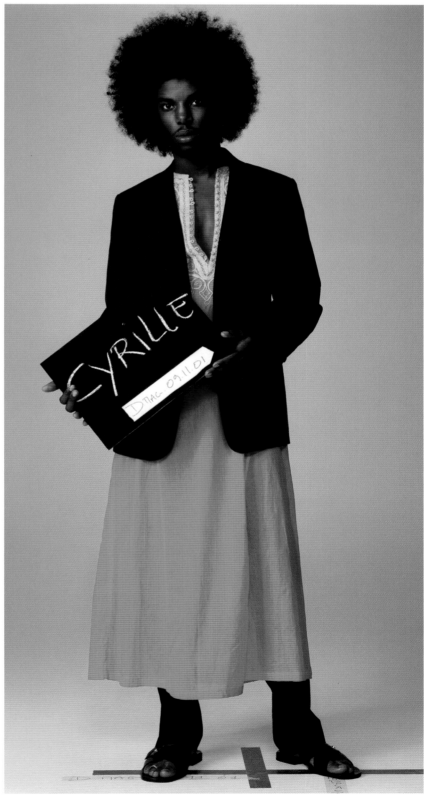

left: **Group of men, West Pakistan, 1948**
Photograph courtesy of Henri Cartier-Bresson/Magnum

above: **Giorgio Armani, Spring/Summer 1994**
Photograph courtesy of Maria Valentino/ MCV Photo

opposite: **Photograph by John Akehurst**
for *The Face*, 1996
Styled by Polly Banks
Courtesy of John Akehurst/CLM London

LONG SHIRTS

Similar in cut and appearance to the caftan is the long shirt worn by both
men and women in several parts of the South Asian subcontinent
(above). Usually referred to as either the *kurta* or *qamis* (kameez), it is
traditionally made up of five different parts, known as *asteen* or the sleeves,
daman or the skirt, *kali* or the side pieces, *baghal* or the gussets under
the armpits, and *gireban* or collar.[25] Originally an undergarment, the *qamis*
developed into a fashionable garment for outerwear in the nineteenth
century. At this time, it developed some of its distinguishing features like
a round neck with a continuing deep slit either in the middle or at the
sides of the neck, at the right or left.[26] The length of the *qamis* varies to
anywhere between the hips to just below the knees. While it can be
worn over a waistcloth, it is more generally worn over a pair of loose
trousers called *paijama* or *salwar/shalwar*. Today, the *salwar* and *qamis* is
the everyday garb of men in Pakistan and other parts of Northern India.
Usually made from white or cream cotton or muslin, the *qamis* resembles
a modern, Western shirt with a turned collar and short cuffs that are split
and buttoned. Generally knee- or calf-length, it has no side pieces but
is cut straight from the armpits. In order that its uniformly wide skirt may
not hinder the free movement of the body, especially while sitting down,
it is slit on the sides from the bottom up to the waistline.

In Britain, second- and third-generation Indian and Pakistani men
wear the *qamis* with jeans or tracksuit bottoms and trainers (right).
It was a look that was promoted in magazines like *Second Generation* and,
although originally a visual representation of 'yellow pride', was adopted
by non-Asian men on the London club scene in the mid- to late-1990s.
More mainstream magazines such as *i-D*, *Arena* and *The Face* promoted
similar looks. In its Spring/Summer 1994 issue, *Arena Homme Plus*
ran a photographic shoot called 'East Side Story', with the by-line,
'Fashion's reference points have never been so diverse: ideas and imagery
are assimilated from eclectic cultural sources. In London's East End,

a unique home-brew of traditional and urban attire has created a new fashion topography.'[27] As well as showing 'authentic' qamis, the shoot included fashionable versions by Katherine Hamnett, Joe Casely-Hayford and Polo Ralph Lauren. Like the qamis worn by second and third generation Indian and Pakistani men, they were combined with designer jackets and shoes.

A number of designers produced versions of the qamis for their Spring/Summer 1994 collections. Giorgio Armani, for instance, showed several versions with linen suits in the natural, stone-beige colours he favours (page 82). The qamis, like his waistcloths mentioned earlier, typify Armani's design mantra of ease and simplicity. In a way, it is an extension of the famous unconstructed jacket he designed in the 1970s. With its breezy informality, the jacket, which was also inspired by regional styles, revolutionized menswear at the time. 'Armani, quite literally, ripped the guts out of what most men had been wearing for generations', comments Patrick McCarthy in 'The Menswear Revolution' (2000). 'Gone were the linings and the padding and the shoulders. In their place was a light-as-a-feather jacket of remarkable simplicity and elegance with sloped shoulders, narrow lapels, and a new, long length.'[28] Like his jacket, Armani's qamis, with its shaping achieved almost exclusively through the hang of the fabric, results in an almost fluid expression of the body.

Jean Paul Gaultier showed two-piece suits with the qamis for his Spring/Summer 1995 collection (below). Like Armani's version, the qamis, reflective of its origins, conveys the impression of a relaxed informality. Although the suit may at first appear conservative, Gaultier's characteristic wit and irony can be seen in his use of such whimsical accessories as a cloche-style hat, a blousy, poppy corsage and a pair of flamboyantly high platform sandals. In the same collection, Gaultier showed a more structured suit with a qamis ostentatiously encrusted in sequins and gemstones, 'frosting' more characteristic of Indian saris than the traditional male qamis.

While Roy Krejberg for Kenzo has also shown the qamis with a two-piece suit, he similarly advocates its use as street wear by combining it with puffa jackets (below right). Likewise, Miguel Adrover for his Spring/Summer 2003 collection showed a qamis paired with shorts, flip-flops and baseball caps. Although the collection, entitled 'Citizen of the World', was inspired by the New York immigrant experience, Adrover's mixing of Western and non-Western signifiers highlighted the universality of such symbols in an early 21st-century context. For his Spring/Summer 2004 collection, Raf Simons combined the qamis, shown under a baggy sweater, with another universal garment of Indian origin, the paisley shawl (below centre).

left: **Jean Paul Gaultier, Spring/Summer 1995**
Photograph courtesy of Maria Valentino/MCV Photo

middle: **Raf Simons, Spring/Summer 2004**
Photograph courtesy of Maria Valentino/MCV Photo

right: **Kenzo advertising campaign,
Autumn/Winter 1999–2000**
Courtesy of Kenzo

opposite: **Sir Ranbir Singh,
Maharajah of Jind (1879-1948)**
Courtesy of The British Library,
Oriental and India Office Collection

GOWNS

The British East India Company
was responsible for promoting what
is perhaps the only skirted garment
commonly worn by men today, the
dressing gown. Since its introduction
in the sixteenth century, the dressing
gown has functioned primarily as
déshabillé or 'undress', casual,
informal dress worn in the private
or semi-private space of the home.
Traditionally a long, loose garment,
it was originally worn for ease
and comfort, usually over the shirt
and doublet or waistcoat in place
of more formal covering. In contrast
to the blandness and uniformity
that characterized much of men's
formal and semi-formal dress after
the Great Masculine Renunciation,
the dressing gown is one of the
few garments in a man's wardrobe
that retains the rich colours,
exuberant patterns and sumptuous
materials associated with
eighteenth-century menswear.
This 'state of grace' may, in part,
explain its popularity among men,
even today.

In the eighteenth century,
the dressing gown was known as
the 'India' gown or, more typically,
the 'banyan'. The term banyan
derives from *banian*, the name
for a Hindu trader hailing from the
province of Gujerat. Officials
or servants of the British East India
Company often relied on the
banian as 'an agent who acted
as his steward, man of affairs,
broker, etc., and who was in theory
his dependent'.[29] The loose
gowns exported to England and
the continent of Europe by
the British East India Company,
often in a style known as the
chogha, became the model
for eighteenth-century banyans.
A sumptuous, long-sleeved,
open-fronted gown, the *chogha*
was traditionally an outer garment
worn by princes and noble
men at court (above). Indeed,
its function as a garment of
rank, status or wealth is clear
from the use of expensive
and extravagant materials.

The banyan was one of the most popular forms of men's dress in the eighteenth century, largely because it afforded the wearer an escape from the closely tailored costume of the time. During the first part of the eighteenth century, the banyan was cut more like a *chogha*, that is to say, in a T-shape with minimal shaping. The second part of the century, however, saw closer tailoring applied to the banyan. Losing some of the comfort associated with the earlier, more commodious style, the banyan began to follow the general cut of the contemporary formal coat.[30] Although worn in the privacy of the home as undress, it was also a permissible form of apparel in which to receive visitors. 'The banyan was a paradigm of men's clothing that was neither bedclothes nor acceptable street apparel,' comment Richard Martin and Harold Koda in *Orientalism: Visions of the East in Western Dress* (1994). However, in the late eighteenth century, there was a vogue for wearing the banyan in public, as is revealed by an extract from the *Town and Country Magazine* for 1785:

'Banyans are worn in every part of the town from Wapping to Westminster, and if a sword is occasionally put on it sticks out of the middle of the slit behind. This however is the fashion, the ton, and what can a man do? He must wear a banyan.'[31]

The many references in both literature and portraiture attest to the banyan's importance in eighteenth-century culture. In portraiture, it is a convention indicating the sitter's literary and philosophical leanings (below). In order to be depicted in the style of gentlemanly ease, Samuel Pepys hired a golden-brown silk banyan when he sat to John Hales in 1666. Despite vibrant colours and patterns, this loosely draped, untailored style of dress was thought to bestow some of the timeless dignity of classical antiquity on the sitter.

In the tradition of the banyan, men's dressing or lounging gowns of the nineteenth century also drew on 'exotic' sources. Although Indian influences were still predominant, most notably in the use of paisley motives, Chinoiserie and Japonisme were also very much in evidence. Many dressing or lounging gowns, for instance, were styled after traditional Chinese and Japanese garments like the dragon robe or the kimono (opposite). Like the Indian *chogha*, both the Chinese dragon robe and the Japanese kimono are T-shaped garments that utilize standard fabric widths sewn together with the minimum of cutting. The dragon robe

Joseph Sherburne, *John Singleton Copley*, c.1767–70
The Metropolitan Museum of Art,
Amelia B. Lazarus Fund, 1923 (23.143)

Koryusai, *A Young Man Accosted by a Courtesan*
Woodblock print, Japan (Edo), early 1770s
V&A:E.2660-1909

overleaf
left: **Photograph by Albert Watson for *Arena*, 2001**
Styled by Allan Kennedy
Courtesy of Albert Watson

right: **Gucci by Tom Ford, Spring/Summer 2003**
Photograph courtesy of Alex Cayley/Creative Exchange

left: **Versace, Spring/Summer 1998**
Photograph courtesy of Maria Valentino/MCV Photo

right: **Shirtology, Spring/Summer 2001**
Courtesy of *Uomo Collezione*

opposite: **Zhou Enlai, Tianjin, China, July 1914**
Photograph courtesy of Beijing, Central Party Literature
Publishing House ©1998

fastens to the side with a series of loops and toggles or buttons. By contrast, the kimono is an open-fronted, crossover gown that is worn wrapped around the body and secured at the waist by a sash or *obi*. Both the kimono and the dragon robe, however, are long, flowing, voluminous garments that are ideally suited to undress or *déshabillé*. Their rich fabrics and, in the case of the dragon robe, ornate decoration, also promote their status as informal 'at home' attire. In the nineteenth century, some men, usually artists and writers, wore authentic kimonos or dragon robes as dressing or lounging gowns. The kimono, for instance, was promoted as informal and semi-formal wear in England by the Aesthetic Movement. Most men, however, wore modified versions or Western re-interpretations of kimonos and dragon robes. In Britain during the nineteenth century, to wear either an authentic or customized dragon robe was not a fanciful or frivolous gesture, but an imperial act signifying worldly knowledge.[32]

In the twentieth century, the kimono or kimono-inspired garment, in particular, remained in use as undress or *déshabillé*. Men stationed on the Pacific Front during the Second World War and later during the Korean War sent kimonos home to the United States, where again they were worn as dressing or lounging gowns. Kimonos have also been a source of inspiration for stylists, designers and photographers (page 88). Tom Ford for Gucci, for instance, created a range of kimonos for his Spring/Summer 2003 collection (page 89). While traditionally men's kimonos are relatively subdued in colour and pattern, Tom Ford produced versions in vivid reds, blues and yellows. Printed with blousy chrysanthemums, Ford's designs were more typical of kimonos traditionally worn by Japanese women. Donatella Versace also produced a range of kimono-inspired garments for her Spring/Summer 1998 collection (above left). She too created versions in vibrant reds and yellows, although they were much shorter, falling to the knee or just below. These versions more resembled the short robe or *haori* worn by both men and women in Japan. When worn by men they are usually sported with a pair of loose trousers or *hakama* open half way down the sides and resembling a divided skirt with six pleats in the front and two pleats in the back.[33] On the runway, however, Versace showed her *haori*-like garments with nothing but swimming trunks. As the models strutted down the catwalk, their garments fell open in a deliberate act of sexual provocation. Shirtology produced even shorter versions for its Spring/Summer 2001 collection (above right). Made out of transparent fabric to reveal the whole torso, this was extreme *déshabillé*.

Dragon robes were originally designed to expand the area around the wearer and thus obscure the body. While narrower, the robes traditionally worn by men in China as everyday wear were also intended to obscure the human form. Known as *changshan*, they were often paired with short riding jackets, adding to the apparent size of the body (right).

The *changshan* was the inspiration behind a series of ensembles designed by Jean Paul Gaultier for his Autumn/Winter 1996–7 collection (opposite). Typical of his iconoclasm, however, Gaultier produced extremely narrow versions made from stretch fabrics that clung to the body and resembled the tight-fitting *qipao* or *cheongsam* made famous by Shanghai starlets in the 1920s and 1930s. On the catwalk he paired his gowns with flared trousers and such foppish accessories as fans and long cigarette holders. It was a look that reprised an image of Sir Sacheverell Sitwell taken by Cecil Beaton in 1927 (above). Sitwell is shown wearing a luxurious dressing gown worn over a shirt and tie, an image that was popularized a year earlier in Marcel L'Herbier's film *Le Vertige* ('Giddiness'), in which the slick-haired Jacque-Catelain pranced through Robert Mallet-Stevens' sets dressed in a sumptuous dressing gown worn over full evening dress.[34] Recently, Ralph Lauren showed a similar look in his Autumn/Winter 2002–3 collection (right). In showing models in dressing gowns with evening dress underneath, however, Lauren was referencing the original function of the banyan, to promote ease and comfort for the gentleman at home.

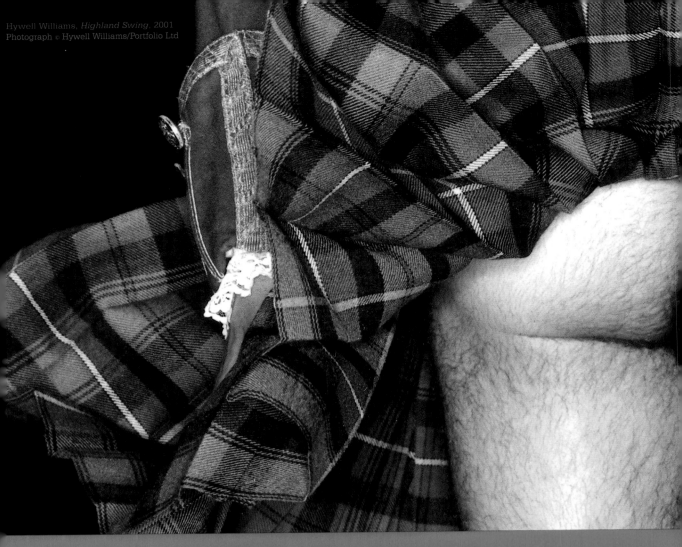

THE KILT

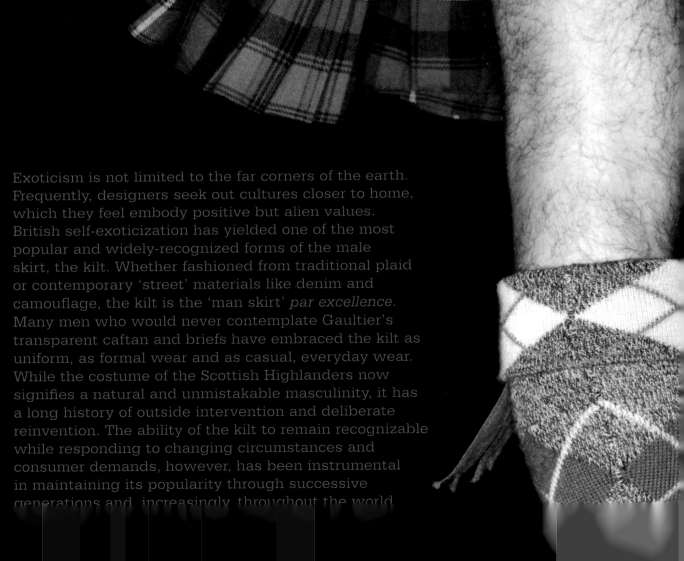

Exoticism is not limited to the far corners of the earth.
Frequently, designers seek out cultures closer to home,
which they feel embody positive but alien values.
British self-exoticization has yielded one of the most
popular and widely-recognized forms of the male
skirt, the kilt. Whether fashioned from traditional plaid
or contemporary 'street' materials like denim and
camouflage, the kilt is the 'man skirt' *par excellence*.
Many men who would never contemplate Gaultier's
transparent caftan and briefs have embraced the kilt as
uniform, as formal wear and as casual, everyday wear.
While the costume of the Scottish Highlanders now
signifies a natural and unmistakable masculinity, it has
a long history of outside intervention and deliberate
reinvention. The ability of the kilt to remain recognizable
while responding to changing circumstances and
consumer demands, however, has been instrumental
in maintaining its popularity through successive
generations and, increasingly, throughout the world.

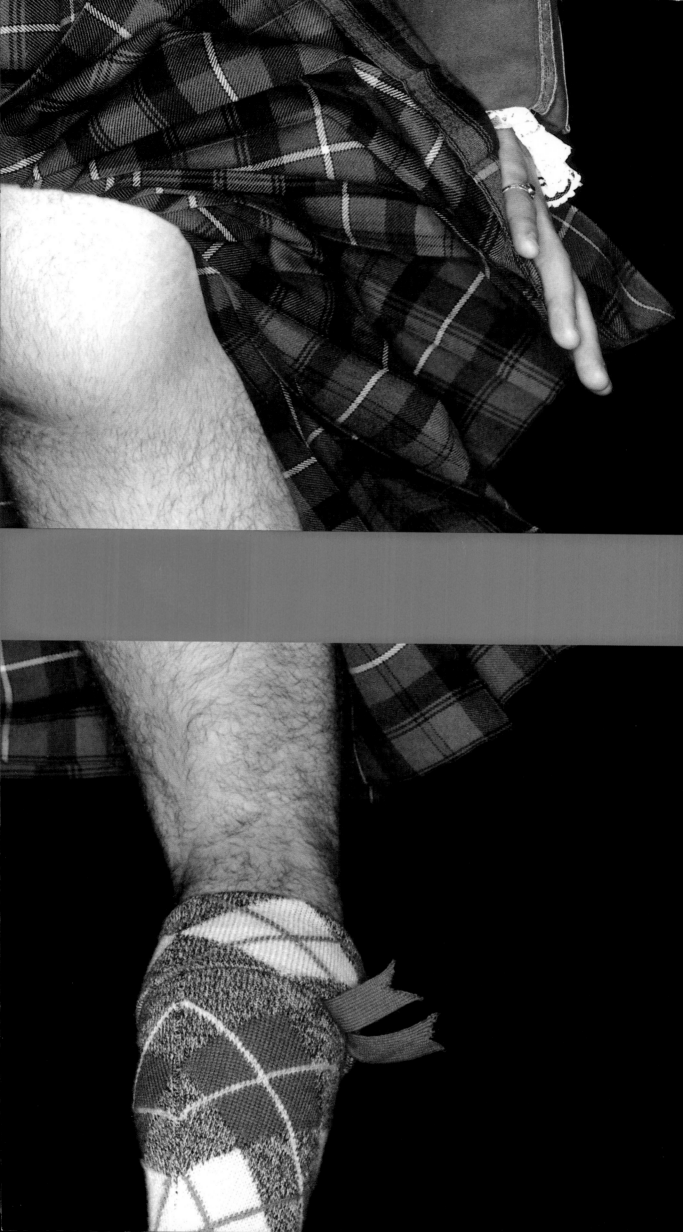

John Michael Wright, *Sir Mungo Murray*
Oil on canvas, c.1683
Courtesy of Scottish National Portrait Gallery

FORM AND EVOLUTION

The kilt as we know it today originated in the first quarter of the eighteenth century. Known to the Gaelic-speaking Highlander as the 'little wrap' (*feileadh beag*), it evolved from the 'big wrap' or belted plaid (*feileadh mor*), the first identifiably and, therefore, authentically 'Scottish' costume that emerged in the late sixteenth century. Earlier, the Scottish Gaels had worn the same clothes as their Irish counterparts, namely a shirt known in Gaelic as the *léine* and a semi-circular mantle known in Gaelic as the *brat*. In the *History of Greater Britain* (1521), John Major describes the early sixteenth-century dress of the Highlanders:

'From the middle of the thigh to the foot they have no covering for the leg, clothing themselves with a mantle instead of an upper garment and a shirt dyed with saffron … In time of war they cover their whole body with a shirt of mail or iron rings, and fight in that. The common people of the Highland Scots rush into battle having their body clothed with a linen garment manifoldly sewed and painted or daubed with pitch, with a covering of deerskin.'[1]

For Major, the distinguishing feature of the appearance of the Highlanders was bare knees and the ready possibility of large-scale exposure of the lower body. With the replacement of the brat-and-léine with the belted plaid or *feileadh mor*, bare knees remained the chief signifier of Highland dress, preserving this fundamental continuity.

The belted plaid had a discernible style of its own (above). It was constructed from a large rectangular piece of material about 5 feet wide and roughly 14-16 feet long. Because of the difficulty of weaving a wide web on the old hand loom, it was made up of two lengths of material about 30 inches wide sewn together.[2] Simple, versatile and classless, it served as dress by day and blanket by night. In *Highland Costume* (1977),

John Telfer Dunbar explains how the belted plaid was arranged on the body:

'In order to put it on … the wearer had first to lay it out on the ground. The length of it was then reduced to about 4 or 5 feet by pleating the material over but leaving an unpleated panel about 2 feet wide at each end. The wearer then lay down on top of the plaid, on his back, with one edge of the pleats just above the back of his knees, the pleats being parallel with his spine. He then folded one of the unpleated panels across his stomach, and then the other on top. He was now wearing something like the modern kilt below his waist, and in order to keep it in place he merely girded a belt around his waist and stood up.'[3]

Several dress historians, however, have discounted this method on the grounds of impracticality. They propose that the most pragmatic (and time-effective) method was to gather the pleats in the hand, pass the plaid around the body, secure

it loosely with the belt, then tighten it after a final adjustment of the pleats.[4]

As a set of engravings by Van der Gucht (1740s) reveal, the top half of the belted plaid could be worn in a variety of ways. The most basic arrangement involved the plaid hanging down over the belt at the back and reaching to the calves. Usually, the front was open showing the kilted portion below the belt, falling to just above the knees. Another arrangement involved drawing the plaid over both shoulders. This style was worn to protect the wearer in inclement weather. A third arrangement involved drawing the plaid over one shoulder only, allowing the wearer freedom of action to use the dirk, sword and musket. The little shoulder plaid worn with certain modern Highland dress is a relic of this style.

The kilt as worn today is the lower half of the belted plaid with the back pleats stitched up (above). It was constructed from one of the two lengths of material that made up the belted plaid. Ironically, its invention is credited to an English man, Thomas Rawlinson, who came from a long-established family of Quaker ironmasters in Furness. How Rawlinson came to invent the kilt is explained in a letter by a Mr Baille of Aberiachan, 'a man of good education and position and a member of a Highland family living beside Loch Ness.'[5] Part of the letter, dated 22 March 1768, was published in the *Edinburgh Magazine* in March 1785:

'About 50 years ago, one Thomas Rawlinson, an Englishman, conducted an iron work carried on in the countries of Glengarie and Lochaber; he had a throng of Highlanders employed in the service, and became very fond of the Highland dress, and wore it in the neatest form; which I can aver, as I become personally acquainted with him above 40 years ago. He was a man of genius and quick parts, and thought it no great stretch of invention to abridge the dress, and make it handy and convenient for his workmen: and accordingly directed the using of the lower part plaited of what is called the felie or kilt as above, and the upper part was set aside… It was found so handy and convenient that, in the shortest space, the use of it became frequent in all the Highland Countries, and in many of our northern Low Countries also.'[6]

What is interesting about Mr Baille's account, however, is not the name and nationality of the kilt's inventor, but the motivations behind the kilt's invention. By substituting the belted plaid with the little kilt, Rawlinson's intention was not to preserve the Highlanders' traditional way of life, but to ease its transformation. As Hugh Trevor-Roper comments in his article 'The Invention of Tradition: The Highland Tradition of Scotland' (1983), the little kilt was designed 'to bring [the Highlanders] out of the heather and into the factory.'[7]

ROMANTICISM: THE KILT AS NATIONAL DRESS

Not long after Rawlinson's ingenious innovation, the Diskilting Act was passed in the wake of the Jacobite Uprising of 1745. This rebellion, organized by Prince Charles Edward Stuart (Bonnie Prince Charlie), marked the final attempt by the Jacobites to regain the British throne. As in the previous Jacobite risings, the 'Young Pretender' sought and won the support of many Highland chiefs and their clans. When the Jacobites were defeated at the Battle of Culloden (1746) by the Duke of Cumberland and his troops, a campaign of 'pacification' of the Highlands was undertaken 'beginning with fire and the sword, and leading on into social engineering of various kinds.'[8] The latter included the proscription of Highland costume which was seen as a symbol of rebellion and primitive savagery. After a proposed series of Disarming Acts, came the Act of 1746 which decreed:

'...*That from and after the First Day of August, One thousand seven hundred and forty-seven, no Man or Boy, within that part of Great Britain called Scotland, other than such as shall be employed as Officers and Soldiers in His Majesty's Forces, shall, on any Pretence whatsoever, wear or put on the Clothes commonly called Highland Clothes (that is to say) the Plaid, Philebeg, or little Kilt, Trowse, Shoulder Belts, or any Part whatsoever of what peculiarly belongs to the Highland Garb...*'[9]

The penalty for a first offence was six months' imprisonment, and for a second offence, transportation to His Majesty's Plantations for a period of seven years. In *Tartan: The Highland Habit* (1991), Hugh Cheape observes that the strictness of the sanction reflected the serious fear and sense of political threat inspired by the belted plaid and little kilt.[10]

Highlanders were forced to adopt Saxon trousers. In his 'Song to the Breeches' ('Oran do' n Bhriogais'), Duncan Ban Macintyre made the freedom of movement permitted by the plaid into a metaphor for the liberty of the Gael, and the restriction of trousers into a metaphor for their legal subjugation:

'*And since we put the trousers on*
That clothing does not please us well
Pinching us around our houghs
Uncomfortable to wear
Unlucky this new dress of ours,
Uglily does it sit on us,
So tightly does it cling to us,
We'd sooner see no more of it'[11]

The Act proscribing Highland dress had made an exception for those serving in the armed forces. In 1725, Field Marshal George Wade, the Commander-in-Chief in Scotland responsible for demilitarizing the Highlands, raised six 'independent companies' of Highlanders to police the area from which it was recruited and to counter any suspected Jacobite activity. Later, in 1739, these independent companies were formed into a regiment of ten companies and were supplied with a uniform tartan of 'government pattern' in a green, blue and black check. The regiment was called 'Black Watch', their name recalling the 'watch' employed by clans to guard against cattle raiding. When other regiments were raised they distinguished their tartans by adding a line of a different colour to the basic government pattern. Indeed, it is likely that the later practice of differentiating tartan by clans came out of this need to distinguish the uniforms of the different Highland regiments.

Originally, the Highland regiments were dressed in the belted plaid, but in order to conform with the other regiments of the British Army they wore a red coat cut away at the skirts to allow for its voluminous folds (opposite). Other distinctive Highland features of the uniform included a round blue bonnet, a small leather sporran, red and white knee-length hose and black buckled shoes. By about 1810, however, the Highland regiments had replaced the belted plaid with the little kilt. As such, the red coat no longer needed to be altered to allow for the bulk of the belted plaid and the standard jacket worn by other regiments was adopted. At the same time, the small, practical leather sporran developed into a large, hairy, decorative affair. This early nineteenth-century military style was to have a lasting impact on civilian dress. Indeed, several dress historians have claimed that Highland costume would not have survived in civilian form had the Highland regiments not been raised and uniformed in elements of their native dress.

In 1782, through the efforts of the Highland Society of London, the Diskilting Act was repealed. This occasioned great rejoicing in Scotland, with Gaelic poets celebrating the victory of the Celtic belted plaid over the Saxon trousers. In his 'Song to the Highland Garb' ('Oran do 'n Eideadh Ghaidhealach'), Duncan Ban Macintyre wrote:

'We have assumed the suit
That is lightsome and fitting for us
The belted plaid in its pleats...
The Gaels will hold up their heads
And they will be hemmed in no more
Those tight fetters have vanished
That made them languid and frail.' [12]

By the time of the repeal, the kilt had fallen out of use as an item of ordinary dress, allowing for what Malcolm Chapman in *The Celts: The Construction of a Myth* (1992) calls the 'romantic rehabilitation of Highland dress'. [13] The romantic gaze was a reaction against the urban and the industrial and a celebration of the untamed wilderness. No longer the threat from the north, the image of the Highlands could represent this wilderness within the bustling economy of the 'new' Britain. Rather than dangerous, bare-legged barbarians, the Highlanders' became admirable, a kilted version of the noble savage.

      With the near extinction of the kilt came an urgency among the establishment to bring about its revival. After the repeal of the Diskilting Act, the kilt rapidly moved from the periphery to the very centre, accompanied by all the processes of forgetting and imaginative re-creation. [14] The romantic rehabilitation of the kilt reached its high point with King George IV's carefully stage-managed State Visit to Edinburgh in 1822, during which he disported himself in Highland dress. This 'publicity stunt' promoted the kilt as fashionable wear among the Scottish nobility and, in so doing, helped establish the kilt as the national dress of Scotland. Elite validation is critical to the elevation of any item of dress to the status of national dress. As Lou Taylor comments in *The Study of Dress History* (2002), 'The process of inventing a "national" dress usually involves the appropriation of peasant styles as romanticized and utopian icons of democratic struggle and national cultural revival.' [15]

      The King's highly flamboyant visit was organized by Sir Walter Scott with the help of Colonel David Stewart of Garth, who, in 1820, founded the Celtic Society of Edinburgh, a society of young civilians whose first objective was 'to promote the general use of the ancient Highland dress in the Highlands.' [16] Through his writings, Scott himself played an important role in the idealization and romanticization of the Scottish Gaels. His novels *Waverley* (1814) and *Rob Roy* (1818) as well as his narrative poems *Marmion* (1808), *The Lady of the Lake* (1810) and *The Lord of the Isles* (1815) generated enormous public interest in the Scottish Highlands and made their author internationally famous.

      With King George IV's State Visit to Scotland, Scott realized his romantic Celtic fantasies and, in the process, created a lasting impression of the Highlands and Highlanders as 'picturesque'. Assisted by Stewart and other members of the Celtic Club, Scott made the Highlanders central to Scottish historical self-understanding. [17] In what was described by Scott's son-in-law, John Gibson Lockhart, as a 'Celtic hallucination', groups of Highlanders gathered in Edinburgh under the command of their respective chiefs. As one Edinburgh citizen commented, 'Sir Walter Scott has ridiculously made us appear to be a nation of Highlanders, and the bagpipe and the tartan are the order of the day.' [18] The Royal visit did, indeed, plunge the nation into a tartan frenzy, with the number of clan tartans increasing tenfold within three weeks.

      The popularization of clan tartans was driven by commercial factors, developed as they were by manufacturers as a response to the Royal visit. The greatest of these firms was William Wilson and Sons of Bannockburn. Through the efforts of Sir Walter Scott and Colonel David Stewart of Garth, with the help of William Wilson and Sons, Edinburgh was suitably 'tartanized' to receive the first Hanoverian monarch to step foot on Scottish soil. Inspired by Scott's romanticized image of the Highlander as warrior hero, King George himself appeared in full Highland dress at a levée which was held at Holyrood Palace on 17 August and attended by a vast concourse of the Scottish nobility, both Highlanders and Lowlanders, also in full Highland dress (opposite). Before the Diskilting Act, the upper and middle classes of Scotland had reviled the traditional garb of the

Highlanders, which they regarded as a badge of servility. However, during the years of proscription, several Highland noblemen had taken pleasure in wearing the kilt, albeit in the safety of their homes. Immediately after the repeal, only the gentry or the privileged could afford to replace the Saxon trousers with the Celtic kilt. Now, spurred on by Royal patronage, Scottish polite society picked up the kilt with enthusiasm. Their clothes, however, were far removed from those worn by the Highlanders of the previous century. Given the fact that they were largely designed for the levée, assembly and ballroom, the emphasis was on the dramatic and spectacular. As Hugh Cheape points out, '"Highland dress" turned into "tartan costume". A practical dress with style became ... a fashionable dress with little regard for function.'[19]

Throughout the nineteenth century, aristocratic patronage continued to provide cachet for this new urban-based national style. From the 1840s, it was given new impetus through Queen Victoria's cult of the Highlands. The Queen's enthusiasm for the Highlands and Highlanders began with her first visit to Scotland in 1842. Five years later she bought Balmoral, the ownership of which 'reminded her of a remote but tangible connection with the ancient dynasty of the Royal House of Stewart, of the "king over the water", and Bonnie Prince Charlie's desperate and hopeless bid for the throne.'[20] Queen Victoria shared King George IV's romantic vision of Scotland, and looked to the Highlands as a rural, primitive and pre- or non-industrial utopia. During the early years of her reign, the idea of clan tartans was both extended and systematized, largely through the works of James Logan (*Clans of the Scottish Highlands*) and John Sobieski Stolberg Stuart and Charles Edward Stuart (*Vestiarium Scoticum* and *The Costume of the Clans*). Balmoral's interiors reflected the Queen's enthusiasm for tartan and sparked a trend for tartan worldwide that became known as 'Balmoralism'. Victoria herself favored Dress Stewart, a variation of the Royal Stewart tartan in which the broad band of red is changed to white.

Prince Albert shared his wife's passion for Balmoral, leading him to design the Balmoral tartan, first produced in about 1860 for the exclusive use of the Royal Household. The Prince's own adoption of Highland costume did much to further its acceptance by the fashionable elite of Scotland. As a fashionable outfit, Highland costume began to have 'correct' items and styles of wear for day and evening, etiquettes that remain relatively unchanged to this day. Victorian conventions favored as full a range of accoutrements as possible. More decorative than functional, these included dirk, *sgian dubh*, belt plate, plaid brooch, shoe buckles and bonnet badges. Indeed, if King George's visit to Scotland elevated Highland costume to the status of national dress, Queen Victoria's cult of the Highlands effectively brought about its commodification.

RE-CONTEXTUALIZATION

The kilt continues to be worn today as a symbol of national pride and family and clan associations, although its usage tends to be restricted to special events like weddings and formal balls, dinners or receptions. On such occasions, formal Highland dress is worn in the styles and conventions harking back to Victorian aristocratic and bourgeois etiquette. Modern formal Highland costume comprises: jacket or doublet, waistcoat, shirt, tie or jabot, kilt, kilt pin, sporran, *sgian dubh*, knee-length woollen socks,

garters, flashes or ribbons, and patent or lightweight dress shoes, either strapped or of the high-laced ghillie variety. As with much of men's formal wear, specific rules dictate its form. The kilt should sit approximately two inches above the waist and rest at the top of the knee. The sporran should sit in the centre of the kilt, and the kilt pin should be pinned through the front apron only. Hose or stockings should be approximately 2-3 finger widths below the bottom of the kneecap with the flashes or ribbons worn to the outside of the leg.

Until relatively recently, day or informal Highland dress tended to be the preserve of older upper- or middle-class Scotsmen keen to assert or project an image of wealth and leisure. Over the past ten years, however, as Scotland has gained a new level of cultural and political confidence, 'a new generation of [young] radical Scots have reclaimed the wearing of the kilt from the embrace of nearly two hundred years of establishment, commodified gentrification.'[21] The Victorian styles of day and evening wear have given way to contemporary usage. Now, many younger men wear their kilts for everyday use with a T-shirt or

sweater, a denim or leather jacket, trainers or chunky, heavy-soled boots, and woolly socks falling around the ankles. As Lou Taylor observes, 'What we are seeing ... is that after nearly two hundred years, a reclamation of the wearing of the kilt is taking place. This is pulling Scottish "national" dress out of the hands of the old establishment élite. Now young Scotsmen wear their kilts according to their own cultural codes and on their own national identity terms, which includes wearing kilts with T-shirts and trainers.'[22]

The actor Ewan McGregor and the singer Fran Healy of Travis exemplify this new generation of kilt wearers (below). Indeed, in much the same way that King George IV's adoption of the kilt promoted its acceptance as fashionable wear among the Scottish elite of the early nineteenth century, the kilt's adoption by actors and musicians has encouraged its acceptance among Scottish youth of the late twentieth and early twenty-first centuries. And, in much the same way that nineteenth-century kilt-making companies exploited the nobility's adoption of the kilt by developing a wide repertoire of clan tartans, modern-

Ewan McGregor
Photograph by Annie Leibovitz for *Vanity Fair*, 1998
Photograph©Press Images

opposite
left: Samuel L. Jackson at the première of *51st State*, London's West End, November 2001
Photograph by Dave Bennett
Courtesy of Alpha

right: Robbie Williams, Australia, 2001
Photograph by Martin Philbey, ©Redferns

day kilt-making companies are developing new styles and designs. One of the first companies to realize the commercial potential of this new generation of kilt wearers is 21st-Century Kilts (TFCK), founded by Howie Nicholsby in 1996. Based in Edinburgh, TFCK promotes two basic styles: a traditional eight-yard hand-sewn kilt; and a contemporary six-yard machine-sewn kilt. Although the latter is constructed along traditional lines, it is designed to sit on the hips like a pair of jeans. While its hem line depends on the personal preference of the wearer, Nicholsby advises him 'to show a bit of knee'.[23] Other design features include the use of Velcro® as a method of fastening and a hidden inside pocket for cash, credit cards and mobile phones. Detachable cargo or combat pockets are optional, as is a back pocket designed to carry a palm computer.

Undoubtedly, however, what the new generation of Scotsmen finds most appealing about Nicholsby's kilts are the fabrics. Discarding clan tartans, Nicholsby offers five different types of fabric: Basic Black; Auld Reekie Tweed; Indigo Denim; Urban Camouflage; and Imitation Leather. As Nicholsby comments, 'I grew up wearing a range of different tartans as we have no family tartan. When I decided to go into the kilt-making business, I determined to make kilts in modern materials in an attempt to take the kilt back to its original purpose – to be a functional, everyday piece of clothing.'[24] Through his use of modern materials, however, Nicholsby has effectively changed the meaning and symbolism of the kilt. As Nicholsby states, 'Taking away the tartan equation from kilts opens this comfortable, versatile garment to all men the world over.'[25]

As we have already seen, the adoption of the kilt by non-Scotsmen is by no means a new phenomenon. Indeed, its appropriation by youth and counter-cultural figures has a long history in both Britain and America. From the mid-1990s, however, the kilt has become increasingly popular among young men wishing to project a self-confidently fashionable image. This can be attributed, at least in part, to the immense success of such films as *Rob Roy* (1995) and *Braveheart* (1995). In the tradition of the romantic movement of the late eighteenth and early nineteenth centuries, these films portray the Highlander as warrior hero and primitive outsider, embodying timeless, masculine values. This image has been reinforced in the arena of sport, most obviously through the Highland Games, now broadcast around the world. In events such as putting the shot, tossing the caber, and throwing the weight, they show men of obvious stamina competing in kilts. Most recently, however, the Highlander as a *beau-ideal* has been promoted by Scottish football supporters (page 105). Their tribal antics and kilted uniform received widespread publicity in France during the World Cup in the summer of 1998, inspiring several fashion shoots in magazines such as *L'Uomo Vogue Sport* (overleaf). Through such images, the kilt has come to represent a ready access to Highland male sexuality. For the non-Scotsman, it provides the means of asserting a self-consciously yet unambiguously masculine persona.

Contemporary designers have drawn heavily on the kilt's hyper-masculine connotations in their attempts to appeal to the young fashion-conscious male. On the catwalk, the kilt is often styled with traditionally masculine

opposite: **Kilt by Scotch House**
Photograph by Koto Bolofo for
L'Uomo Vogue Sport, 2001
Styled by Nikki Brewster
Courtesy of Koto Bolofo/Z-Photographic

right: **Scottish football fan**
Trafalgar Square, London, 1996
Photograph courtesy of Chris Steele-Perkins/
Magnum Photos

overleaf: **Tommy Hilfiger advertising campaign,
Autumn/Winter 1997–8**
Photograph by Mike Toth
Courtesy of Tommy Hilfiger Corporation

props or accessories. For instance, Roberto Menichetti for Burberry Psorsum
showed a kilt paired with chunky socks, thick-soled brogues and a brown
leather jacket for his Autumn/Winter 2000–2001 collection (page 115).
The kilt itself was made in the Burberry Check™, with a blue instead
of the traditional camel colourway. Similarly, Tommy Hilfiger showed a kilt
paired with white sports socks and heavy black biker boots during the
presentation of his Autumn/Winter 1999–2000 collection. Earlier, Hilfiger's
photographic campaign advertising his Autumn/Winter 1997–8 collection
showed a group of multi-ethnic men existing in a kind of edenic space of
homo-social cameraderie (overleaf). The models were depicted wearing their
kilts with plaid shirts and workboots, thus combining two stereotypes of
masculinity, the Highlander and the Lumberjack. While not national dress,
the plaid shirt and workboots (usually worn with jeans) are traditional
signifiers of blue-collar America. Within the United States, they carry certain
cultural specificity, while outside the United States they present and
represent 'Americanness' to the rest of the world. This mixing of national

left: **Jean Paul Gaultier**
Photograph by Jean-Marie Périer for French *Elle*, 1994
Courtesy of Jean-Marie Périer/Sylvie Flaure

above: **Vivienne Westwood, Autumn/Winter 2000–2001**
Photograph by Randall Mesdon for *aRUDE*, 2000
Styled by Miles Cockfield
Courtesy of Randall Mesdon/Creative Exchange

identity symbols can also be seen in Jean Paul Gaultier's 'uniform' of kilt, breton shirt and black biker boots (opposite). Worn by sailors in the French navy, the breton shirt is as potent a symbol of 'Frenchness' as the Eiffel Tower.

Stylists and photographers have also looked to the Highlander as warrior hero as a source of inspiration for their fashion editorials. Like designers, they often accessorize the kilt with traditionally masculine accessories such as leather or denim jackets and the staple heavy, chunky boots. Usually, the models are themselves presented as specimens of consummate manliness, with short, cropped hair and hard, well-toned bodies. Often shirtless with their rippling muscles exposed, they are often engaged in sports like rugby, football and even shadow boxing (above). Another popular stereotype of the kilted male that stylists and photographers draw upon is the aristocratic fop, as typified by the Scottish laird and his English equivalent. The models chosen to represent this stereotype could not be more different than those selected to symbolize the Highlander as warrior hero. Fine-boned with high foreheads and thick, swept-back hair, they are generally portrayed in an arrogant stance with

an expression of élite difference (above, left and right). Far from topless, their torsos are extravagantly swathed in tweed and cashmere with a civilized silk cravat at the neck. Typically located in an idyllic, pastoral setting intended to suggest the vast estate or grounds of the laird, the models are generally photographed participating in such gentlemanly pursuits as hunting, shooting and fishing.

Vivienne Westwood has drawn heavily on this stereotype of the kilted male as a design source. Well-known for her fascination with the British royal family, Westwood has looked in particular to the figure of King George IV for her inspiration. The fanciful tartan costumes which the monarch both wore and popularized, costumes which Hugh Trevor-Roper has referred to as 'a bizarre travesty of Scottish history' [26] have, in

Westwood's hands, become highly whimsical and fantastical parodies of early nineteenth-century élite styles (opposite). While it is ironic that King George IV, who played such a crucial and prominent role in the romanticization of the Highlanders, has himself become the subject of the romantic gaze, such reversals are typical of Westwood's witty and sardonic approach to design. Like George IV, Westwood appreciates the powerful

left: **A traditional Scottish kilt**
Photograph by Mark Lebon for *The Sunday Times*, mid-1980s
Styled by Ralph Shandyliar
Courtesy of Mark Lebon

above: **Kilts by Westaway and Westaway**
Photograph by Richard Croft for *Arena*, 1987
Styled by Simon Foxton
Courtesy of Richard Croft

right: **Vivienne Westwood, Autumn/Winter 1999–2000**
Photograph courtesy of Maria Valentino/MCV Photo

visual attraction in tartan, understanding that its essence is display. And like Prince Albert, whose passion for both the Highlands and Highlanders led him to invent the 'Balmoral' tartan, Westwood's highly dramatic and spectacle-driven ensembles are often made up of a sett or pattern of her own creation, such as 'McBrick' tartan, which is based on the colours of the streets and buildings of London (below). These she often combines with other regional patterns such as Argyle and Fair Isle, the results of which recall the riotously flamboyant ensembles of another British monarch, the hyper-fashionable King Edward VIII, who

later became the Duke of Windsor (opposite left). The Duke mixed patterns and textures with gay abandon, prompting American *Vogue* to comment, 'He has…his own manner of putting things together, contrasting checks with stripes, bold color with bolder color … all in a hundred combinations of improbable elegance.'[27]
In a well-known photograph by Charles Sweel, the Duke is depicted wearing a kilt in Royal Stewart tartan paired audaciously with a black-and-white houndstooth-checked Harris tweed jacket and waistcoat (opposite right). The Duke often wore a kilt for both day and evening wear, favouring

Balmoral, Rothesay, Royal Stewart, Hunting Stewart and Lord of the Isles tartan. In his treatise on fashion entitled *A Family Album*, the Duke described how he triggered a vogue for tartan in the 1950s, a vogue that extended to 'every sort of masculine garment, from dinner jackets and cummerbunds to swimming trunks and beach shorts.'[28] The Duke also did much to popularize the kilt during his lifetime, extending its appeal beyond courtly, aristocratic and bourgeois circles.

Like King George IV and Prince Albert before him, it was the Duke of Windsor's royal status that helped promote the kilt's adoption

by both Scotsmen and non-Scotsmen alike. While existing male members of the House of Windsor have continued the tradition of wearing the kilt, young fashionable men are more likely to wear the kilt if it is worn by their pop or Hollywood icons. We have seen already how Ewan McGregor and Fran Healy of Travis have aided the kilt's adoption among a new generation of Scotsmen. The British singer Robbie Williams and the African-American actor Samuel L. Jackson have similarly endorsed and encouraged its adoption among young, fashionable men from a broad variety of backgrounds (page 103). Samuel L. Jackson wore a kilt for his role as Elmo McElroy in Ronny Yu's action film *Formula 51* or *The 51st State* (2001). Set in contemporary Liverpool, Jackson's choice of attire is constantly referred to throughout the film as a 'skirt' or a 'dress'. While Scotsmen are emphatic in their assertion that the kilt is not a skirt, often citing its unique construction and its position as Scottish national dress as rationale, its status is perceived quite differently outside Scotland, especially when worn by a non-Scotsmen in a non-Scottish context. The simple fact that the kilt is not parted at the crotch qualifies it as a 'skirt' in the eyes of many non-Scotsmen.

left: **Vivienne Westwood, Autumn/Winter 1997–8**
Photograph by Davide Cernuschi for *Harper's Bazaar Italia Uomo,* 1997
Courtesy of Davide Cernuschi

below: **Vivienne Westwood, Autumn/Winter 2002–3**
Courtesy of Maria Valentino/MCV Photo

right: **Edward, Prince of Wales, in Scotland, 1934**
Photograph by Charles Sweel
Courtesy of Sotheby's, NY

left to right:
Burberry Prorsum, Autumn/Winter 2000–2001
Courtesy of Burberry
Dries van Noten, Spring/Summer 2000
Photograph by Pascal Therme
Courtesy of Dries van Noten
Pringle of Scotland by Stuart Stockdale,
Spring/Summer 2003
Photograph courtesy of Pringle of Scotland

opposite: Jigsaw Menswear advertising campaign,
Autumn/Winter 1998–9
Photograph by Terry Richardson
Courtesy of Jigsaw Menswear

overleaf: Y's by Yohji Yamamoto, Spring/Summer 2001
Photograph by Sophie Delaporte for i-D, 2001
Styled by Karl Plewka
Courtesy of Sophie Delaporte/Michele Filomeno, Paris

Various designers have attempted to blur the lines between kilt and skirt by re-working elements of the kilt's design. Like Howie Nicholsby, they have most typically focused their efforts on foregrounding the cut over the culturally-specific tartan. For instance, Chris Bailey for Jigsaw Menswear Autumn/Winter 1998–9 collection produced kilts in grey and black wool (opposite). As Bailey comments, 'I wanted to update and modernize the kilt by stripping it of its traditional tartan and replacing it with solid, yet masculine colorways. It was my attempt to take the kilt out of Scotland and place it within a contemporary urban environment.'[29] Bailey, like Nicholsby, wanted his kilts to appeal to a wide customer base, hence his decision to style his kilts with such masculine accessories as denim jackets and hobnail boots. 'While I wanted to tackle the idea of a man in a skirt,' Bailey argues, 'I also wanted to make it appealing to the young, fashion-conscious man. For me the challenge was to create a garment that was both accessible and acceptable to the modern male, rather than a future, imagined male.'[30] While the Jigsaw line was successful in a limited edition, it also served to radicalize the company's identity. As with most branded design, it was an exercise in generating cachet. In other words, these skirts sold trousers.

The process of eschewing tartan in favour of monochromatic colours can also be seen in the work of Dries van Noten. For his Spring/Summer 2000 collection he presented a range of kilts in red, black and white (above). Worn over faded jeans and paired with woollen vests, the models strutted down the catwalk with cropped hair and tribal make-up carrying baseball bats. This threatening and emphatically masculine look not only referenced the barbarism of the mythic Highlander warrior, but also

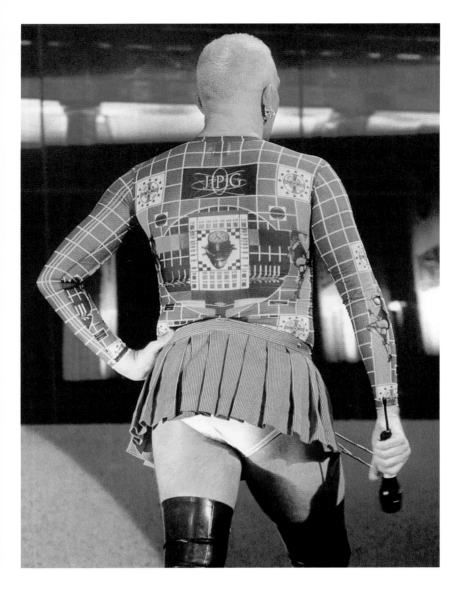

left: **Jean Paul Gaultier**
Photograph courtesy of Dave Hogan

right: **Street performer in Covent Garden, London**
Photograph by David Simon for *Street*, 2000
Courtesy of *Street*

opposite: **Workman's kilt by Utilikilts**
Courtesy of Utilikilts

the tribalism of the Punk Rocker. While constructed along traditional lines, the kilts themselves were made from cotton. Fastened by a plain canvas tape attached to a frayed waistband, the overriding impression was one of primitivism mixed with an air of contemporaneity. As Dries van Noten comments, 'The design of the kilt has remained the same for centuries. In a way it has become almost as conservative as a man's pin-stripe suit. It has to move forward, to change with the times, otherwise it loses its original potency.'[31]

Dries van Noten's use of non-traditional materials, like his use of solid colourways, is another device often used by designers to obfuscate the lines between the kilt and a skirt. Typically, designers favour thick, dense materials that have a masculine feel or, more specifically, that have traditionally masculine associations. Yohji

Yamamoto, for instance, has made kilts in leather (previous pages), while Jean Paul Gaultier and Stuart Stockdale for Pringle of Scotland have made kilts in functional, heavy-duty denim (page 115). Other designers like Vivienne Westwood have used softer, more luxurious fabrics that by modern-day standards have more feminine connotations. For her Autumn/Winter 2001-2 collection, for instance, she designed a range of kilts in chantilly lace. With Westwood's archaeological approach to design, the fact that chantilly lace was a fabric used in sixteenth-, seventeenth- and eighteenth-century aristocratic menswear, most notably in shirts and neckerchiefs, must certainly have affected or prompted her choice of material.

Even while maintaining the cut of the kilt, designers have sought to adapt its length. As noted earlier, the kilt conventionally sits

approximately two inches above the waist and rests at the top of the knee. The kilts produced by most designers, however, rest on the waist while their length can vary enormously. Usually, they fall to just below the knee, although some designers, like Yohji Yamamoto, have made dramatic ankle-length versions. More provocatively, Jean Paul Gaultier has made (and worn) both mini- and micro-kilts (above). John Stephen, the Glasgow-born tailor famous for putting Carnaby Street on the map, designed a mini-kilt as early as 1968. Made from Princess Elizabeth tartan, it reached six inches above the knee and had a large split up the side. Stephen commented at the time, 'Traditional tartans have some magnificent colour blends. All it needed to put them in the style field was the right cut and styling.'[32] While not as overtly sexualizing as Gaultier's designs,

Stephen's kilts were equally as radical in their day. With their exposure of the thigh (and the likely exposure of the genitalia), mini- and micro-kilts may not be a credible option for many men. But within subcultural and performance contexts, they offer men a means of expressing a frank masculinity while simultaneously projecting a self-confidently unconventional persona (page 118).

A more realistic option and one that has proved enormously popular among certain men in America is the 'utilikilt'. Designed by the Seattle-based partnership of Steven Villegas and Megan Haas, the utilikilt emphasizes the masculinity and functionality of the kilt at the expense of most of its other formal qualities. As well as dispensing with the culturally-specific tartan and employing such non-traditional materials as cotton, denim and leather, Villegas and

Haas have also radically altered the kilt's cut and construction. Initially designed for DIY, in its 'Original' version, the utilikilt has a back pocket and two large side 'saddle' pockets analogous to those of cargo or combat trousers. In its 'Workman' version, it incorporates such features as a retractable hammer loop, key-ring and tape-measure loops, saddle pockets with tool pouches, and a 'modesty' snap between the legs for climbing ladders (above). As Villegas comments, 'I created the utilikilt as a comfortable alternative to trousers, something that would enable me to work on my motorcycle. By following the credo "form follows function", I constructed the garment to be worn on an everyday basis, to be easy to care for and, above all, to be durable. By integrating these considerations I believe that we have succeeded in creating a "man-skirt" that is

decidedly masculine and endowed with usable and necessary features.'[33] Utilikilts is one of many crusading organizations promoting the practical advantages of skirts for men. As Villegas observes, 'Our company is driven not by demographics, but by our customers and their needs. It takes balls to wear a skirt, and that is one thing that our customers have in common, whether they drive a tractor, teach college, work in the media, brew beer, or work in construction, every one of them is an innovator.'[34] While this egalitarian reading of the kilt may seem decontextualizing, it still draws on the romanticized image of the Highlander as warrior hero. It seems that the flagrant failure of the Scotsman to adhere to the conventional propriety that men wear trousers and women wear skirts continues to excite the imagination even today.

SUBCULTURAL STYLES

The transgression of gender has a social and even
a political charge that few other forms of self-expression
can match. Various men who have wished to
characterize themselves as resistant, rebellious or
simply contrarian have adopted skirted garments as a
sign of their refusal to meet societal expectations.
Groups of people, who, through their activities and
self-presentations, seek to define themselves in
contradistinction to the parent or mainstream culture,
are known as subcultures. Music has been a focus
of subcultural activity and gender disruption throughout
the twentieth century. In the cultures of jazz and the
blues, certain attributes of femininity such as
elaborate hairstyles, ostentatious jewelry, and luxurious,
flamboyant fabrics, have been badges of subversion
and alternative values since the 1920s.[1] As every
era invents its own street tribes, these strategies are
re-cast and re-played in pointed contrast to what
'straight' or 'normal' society considers the norm.

GLAM ROCK

The deliberate manipulation and blurring of gender distinctions was a core feature of Glam Rock in the 1970s. Moving on from the long hair and exotic fashion styles of Hippies in the 1960s, Glam emphasized androgyny, seeking to unite masculine and feminine qualities in one body. Tapping into the 'nostalgia cult' of the early 1970s, it challenged the boundaries of gender representation by drawing on ideas of sexual glamour from science fiction to the golden age of Hollywood. David Bowie, a central figure in the Glam Rock movement, was particularly successful in constructing a seductive, androgynous persona. In his book *Subculture: The Meaning of Style* (1979), Dick Hebdige writes, '[Bowie] attracted a mass youth (rather than teeny-bopper) audience

and set up a number of visual precedents in terms of personal appearance (make-up, dyed hair, etc.) which created a new sexually ambiguous image for those youngsters willing and brave enough to challenge the notoriously pedestrian stereotypes conventionally available to working-class men and women.'[2] For Bowie, the skirted garment was an obvious target for transgressive styling. In the first of a series of camp incarnations, which later included Ziggy Stardust and Aladdin Sane, Bowie posed in a dress for his 1971 album cover *The Man Who Sold The World* (below left and right). The dress was one of two that Bowie purchased from the British designer Michael Fish, known as Mr Fish, for fifty pounds each. In the late 1960s, Mr Fish had made a mini-skirt, or

rather a 'mini-shirt', which was famously worn by Mick Jagger at the legendary 1969 Rolling Stones concert in Hyde Park, London (page 124). In a lengthy description of the event, Mr Fish explained:

'Mick went into (my shop) Mr Fish to get a white outfit for [Prince Rupert Lowenstein's White Ball].

'I'd made two outfits, one in purple and one in white, for a fashion show at the London Planetarium. One was made for Calvin Lockhart, this most beautiful black actor, and one for Lord Lichfield. The trousers and gillet were moiré, without sleeves. I'd been to Greece for a holiday, and the silhouette that stuck in my mind, which was never seen in this country, was on the soldiers where this extraordinary thing stuck up at the sides and had pom poms.

left: **David Bowie in dress by Michael Fish, 1971**
Photograph by Dennis Stone ©Mirrorpix

right: **David Bowie on the album cover** of *The man who sold the world*, 1971
Courtesy of Jones/Tintoretto Entertainment Co. LLC

I thought "My God! If anyone in England wore that – imagine."

'So I told my designer what I wanted. When it was done, Barry Sainsbury put Patrick (Lichfield) off, saying "You'll look like a big girl's blouse wearing that." Calvin Lockheart also went wobbly. The boy who wore it was a very sweet Scottish shepherd called Stuart. So there was this one white outfit and the purple one (I'd love to know where the purple one is) and in came Mick when I was away and picked it up and probably said, "Can I have it cheap, because it's been worn?" and "Put it on my account" probably, because he's always rather careful. Nothing wrong with being careful.

'The first thing I knew about it was when I came back on the aeroplane from Canada to see a front page: "Where Did You Get That Frock?" Going on, "You can get this frock from Sheila in the King's Road." A line for line copy. Already. Well, I nearly died. You could have knocked me down with a feather.

'Most people think that Ozzie Clark made that outfit, because he was backstage at the gig, and had helped Mick put all the butterflies in the box the night before. Ozzie and I used to laugh about it. He used to say, "Michael, I'm always telling people it's nothing to do with me".'[4]

In his book *Rock/Fashion* (1999) Joshua Sims proclaims, 'By wearing what was essentially a white moiré mini-dress over white trousers … Jagger, his lips smeared with blood-red lipstick, his hair newly washed and hanging over his shoulders, gave a performance of unprecedented sexual ambiguity.'[5] Bowie, who was present at the concert, was heavily influenced by Jagger's 'sexual ambiguity', a theme Jagger explored more thoroughly in his role as the reclusive rock star 'Turner' in Nicholas Roeg's film *Performance* (1970), where again he wore a dress by Mr Fish. Indeed, Jagger's 'brilliant, persona-skipping character'[6] may possibly have been the inspiration for Bowie's Ziggy Stardust and Aladdin Sane.

Bowie's appearance on the album cover of the *Man Who Sold The World*, however, was more Pre-Raphaelite aesthete than the cosmic or extraterrestrial androgyne he was later to affect. In an interview with Cameron Crowe for *Playboy* (1976), Bowie revealed, 'Funnily enough, and you'll never believe me, it was a parody of

Gabriel Rossetti. Slightly askew, obviously.'[7] Indeed, the style of the dress resembled the medieval-style gowns worn by various women in the Aesthetic Movement in the late nineteenth century. Nonetheless, when the album was released in the United Kingdom, Bowie's languid be-frocked figure reclining on a chaise longue draped in blue velvet caused a minor fracas. When journalists asked Bowie why he was wearing a dress, he responded, 'You must understand that it's not a woman's dress. It's a man's dress. The important fact is that I don't have to drag up. I'm just a cosmic yob, I suppose. I've always worn my own style of clothes. I design them. I just don't like the clothes that you buy in shops. I don't wear dresses all the time, either. I change every day. I'm not outrageous. I'm David Bowie.'[8] Kevin Rowland, the ex-lead singer of the British band Dexy's Midnight Runners, repeated the same arguments, with rather less success, when he tried to launch his solo career in 1999 wearing a white mini-dress (above).[9]

In general, the British press regarded Bowie's image as 'just plain silly',[10] but the American press took it more seriously. American journalists regarded it as a direct challenge to traditional values and beliefs about male and female appearance and behaviour, and reported that Bowie 'would prefer to be regarded as a latter-day Garbo', and was 'almost disconcertingly reminiscent of Lauren Bacall.'[11] America had its own proponents of the androgynous look in such Glam Rock acts as Iggy Pop and The New York Dolls who 'proudly wore dresses and slut make-up'.[12] So strong, however, was America's reaction to Bowie's appearance that Mercury, his record label at the time, was forced to change the cover of *The Man Who Sold The World*. As Henry Edwards and Tony Zanetta explain in *Stardust: The David Bowie Story* (1986), 'When the artwork reached Chicago, it was rejected. Conservative American radio stations would never give airplay to songs written by a transvestite.'[13] However, for many male (and female) adolescents, Bowie opened up 'questions of sexual identity which had previously been repressed, ignored or merely hinted at in rock and youth culture.'[14] Nevertheless, by the middle of the decade, youth culture in London and New York was striving for something more confrontational than Bowie's soft-focused Pre-Raphaelite androgyny.

PUNK

The disruptive impact of men in skirts was actively sought by Punk Rockers. Punk's origins lie in the mid-1970s New York underground music scene. As Zeshu Takamura observes in *Roots of Street Style* (1997), 'born amidst the declining musical forces of big-name musicians and the bored pessimism of West coast rock … [Punk] aimed to bring back the original pure passion and energetic beat and style of rock music.'[15] CBGBs, a club in New York's East Village, was instrumental in shaping and promoting Punk Rock through the likes of Blondie and Television. In Britain, Malcolm McLaren drew on and developed American Punk into a peculiarly British phenomenon. Epitomized by McLaren's band the Sex Pistols, British Punk music was more nihilistic than American Punk. In the mid-1970s, Britain was suffering from rising unemployment and the worst economic recession since the 1930s. Punk claimed to speak for the neglected, disaffected and disenfranchised white working-class youth (although, in reality, many Punks were actually middle-class). With its battle cry of 'No Future', British Punk aimed to bring about a new year zero, through a raw do-it-yourself smash-and-grab aesthetic.

As opposed to Glam Rock, Punk's self-representation was abject, aiming to appal and disgust. In a world where the future seemed increasingly hopeless, Punk style reflected an apocalyptic, androgynous tribalism. Make-up to provoke rage and indignation was worn by both boys and girls.

Hair was dyed bright green, orange or yellow and sculpted into warrior-like tufts. Hebdige argues that the 'earthiness of Punk ran directly counter to the arrogance, elegance and verbosity of the Glam Rock superstars.'[16] At the same time, however, like the Glam aesthetic, the Punk aesthetic was one of irony and pastiche. Consequently, Punk represented 'a deliberately scrawled addendum to the "text" of Glam Rock – an addendum designed to punctuate Glam Rock's extravagantly ornate style.'[17]

Vivienne Westwood, in collaboration with Malcolm McLaren, played an important role in the development of Punk style. Westwood and McLaren created the Sex Pistols' look, marketed under their shop label SEX and its successor Seditionaries. The Sex Pistols were intended (at least in part) 'to serve as models for Westwood's latest creations and thereby attract attention to the shop.'[18] Embracing Punk's post-modern ethos of borrowing symbols, imagery and clothing from many epochs and cultures, Westwood created what she called 'confrontation dressing'.[19] Together with McLaren, she was responsible for formulating the quintessential Punk outfit, which consisted of a pair of bondage trousers worn with either a bondage jacket or parachute shirt, or a mohair jumper, T-shirt or muslin shirt with an obscene image or slogan. Designed to be worn by both men and women, Westwood's bondage trousers epitomized the nihilism, narcissism and, most notably, gender confusion that motivated Punk fashion.

Westwood and McLaren collaborated on the conception and construction of the bondage trousers. As Jane Mulvagh describes in *Vivienne Westwood: An Unfashionable Life* (1998):

'McLaren had brought some standard-issue cotton army trousers back from the United States, which Vivienne copied in shiny black sateen McLaren had seen on the back of British Rail clerks' waistcoats and sourced in Manchester. It was McLaren's idea to add the bondage straps between the knees, an extension of the trussed-up sexual look they had purveyed in SEX. They discussed which tribal appendage could be added to these utilitarian trousers, settling on the loincloths worn by primitive tribesmen. Vivienne insisted that their version of this – the "bum flap" – should be in toweling. She added her characteristically finicky "couture" details: zips down the legs (allowing the trousers either to flap around the calves or cling tightly to them) and a fetishist zip that ran right under the crutch, from the pubic bone to the coccyx.'[20]

Although originally made in shiny black sateen, Westwood went on to produce bondage trousers in durable tartan wool, a fabric that was to become closely associated with her later work, particularly her 'Anglomania' label, a diffusion line of unisex clothes launched in 1998. The bum flap evolved into a pleated apron that was worn at the front and back of the trousers, and began to resemble a kilt, a detail that enhanced the anarchic and aggressively androgynous image of Punk style (above). The

inspiration for the kilt-like apron came from a girl named Jordan, one of the leading protagonists of the Punk movement. As Mulvagh mentions, 'Jordan had worn a mini tartan kilt, which Vivienne copied, observing in a television interview that it was "reminiscent of a Greek peasant costume".'[21]

In the 1980s, Westwood licensed the design of her bondage trousers, along with her T-shirt designs, to the King's Road boutique 'BOY', established by John Krivine and Stephan Raynor in the late 1970s. BOY's copies, usually made from cotton with wide knee-length skirts, were cheaper than those sold at

Seditionaries and proved to be enormously successful. As Paul Burgess and Alan Parker observe in *Satellite* (1999), BOY 'became the tabloid face of Punk and a huge tourist attraction.'[22] In its mail order catalogues, BOY's bondage trousers were often paired with cropped, sleeveless T-shirts to underscore their rough trade appeal.

Bondage trousers with pleated skirt-like aprons have become one of the most enduring symbols of Punk style (page 127). While certain designers have re-visited them over the years, they have not always managed to imbue them with fresh significance. The American designer Anna Sui, however, whose approach to design

resembles Punk's post-modern do-it-yourself ethos, used them particularly successfully in her Spring/Summer 1994 'Cyberpunk' collection (page 126). Although she retained their original form, she employed the fabrics of science fiction. In so doing, Sui gave birth to a new hybrid, a techno-fetishistic androgyne located in virtual reality.

As a street style, bondage trousers remain ubiquitous among Punks in Europe, most notably in France and Germany where Punk's anti-bourgeois rhetoric has always had a special appeal. Indeed, as a tribal look, Punk survives remarkably unchanged wherever rebellion can be fomented on the cheap (above).

left: **Punks at a pop festival, England, 1983**
Photograph by Henry Grant
Courtesy of The Museum of London

right: **Steve Strange, 1984**
Photograph courtesy of The Blitz Kids

NEW ROMANTICS

The New Romantics combined the flamboyant decadence of Glam and the post-modern styling of Punk with a new historicism. Maintaining the ability to shock and cause outrage, men played with the theatricality of skirts that brought together exotic and historical styles. The New Romantic movement developed out of the late 1970s London club scene. Its leading proponents were Steve Strange (above), George O'Dowd (Boy George) and Chris Sullivan, former punks 'who took more interest in dressing up and clubbing than in formulating an ideology of anarchic revolution.'[23] In his autobiography *Take It Like A Man* (1995), Boy George explains, 'Punk had become a parody of itself, an anti-Establishment uniform, attracting hordes of dickheads who wanted to gob, punch and stamp on flowers. I got beer thrown over me at punk gigs and called a poser because I wore make-up and frills. It was sad because I loved the energy and music of punk. In the beginning it was screaming at us to reject conformity but it had become a joke, right down to the £80 Anarchy T-shirts on sale at Seditionaries.'[24]

The birthplace of the New Romantics was a down-at-heel club in London's Soho called 'Billy's'. Inspired by New York's 'Studio 54', which ran different clubs for different scenes on different nights of the week, Rusty Egan and Steve Strange opened 'Bowie Night' in Autumn 1978.[25] Held every Tuesday evening, it was soon the haunt of London's 'dress-up kids'. It was particularly popular among fashion students from Central Saint Martin's, who used it as a venue to show off their lavish creations. As Strange explains in his autobiography *Blitzed!* (2002), 'Billy's attracted a clique of outrageous people like a magnet. It was bizarre. All these people were dressed like royalty, while in reality they were just ex-punks running up their clothes on their mum's sewing machines at home in the suburbs or living in the nearby squats in Warren Street and Great Titchfield Street.'[26] A distinctly anti-punk aesthetic emerged, as boys and girls alike substituted 'the elegant for the slovenly, the precious for the vulgar, Dressing Up for Dressing Down.'[27] The music of Bowie, Roxy Music and Kraftwerk was the order of the night. Boy George felt that 'It had more to do with decadent pre-war Berlin than reflecting life on a South London council estate.'[28]

When Bowie Night proved too popular for its small venue, Egan and Strange opened another club-night at 'Blitz', a wine bar in Great Queen Street in Covent Garden 'decorated with images of World War Two, such murals of St Paul's Cathedral under fire and warplanes flying overhead.'[29] Strange operated a strict door policy, vetting people for entry solely according to their looks and clothes. As he explains, 'It was not hard to decide who to let in and who to leave out. People thought they could get in just by looking ridiculous, but that was not the point. I wanted people to

be stylish.'[30] Eager to discover a new youth culture after the demise of Punk, the media seized upon the stylish denizens of the Blitz club, labeling them the 'Cult With No Name', the 'Blitz Kids' and the 'Now Crowd' before settling on the term 'New Romantics'. As Polhemus states in *Street Style: From Sidewalk to Catwalk* (1994), 'A club of Blitz Kids having fun dressing up was in fact transformed by the media into a fully fledged, international subculture defined by a philosophy of "new romanticism" which always seemed a bit of an afterthought.'[31]

New Romantics eschewed sexual distinctions in dress in favor of spectacular and unconventional effects. In *Fashion, Desire and Anxiety* (2001), Rebecca Arnold notes, 'They wore elaborate combinations of real and imagined past styles, painting their faces to enhance fantasy and artifice, their escape from the natural.'[32] Hedonistic and narcissistic, the New Romantics prized individualism. As Strange observes, it was important to stay one step ahead, 'I was constantly looking through history books, old film magazines and design articles, trying to come up with ideas for new images.'[33] Typically, New Romantics combined homemade clothes with articles from boutiques like PX or theatrical costumiers like Charles Fox, both located in Covent Garden. Their aesthetic received widespread visibility through such bands as Visage, Duran Duran, Spandau Ballet, Adam and the Ants and, perhaps most notably, Culture Club. Boy George was their frontman and he epitomized the excess, artifice and outrageousness that

underscored the New Romantic movement. With his bobtails, vivid make-up and, above all, his skirted garments, Boy George pushed the boundaries of accepted male appearance. He delighted in shocking and provoking his audiences with wild, exotic creations usually designed for him by Sue Clowes and Dexter Wong.

Sue Clowes was the designer behind the shop 'The Foundry' in London's Ganton Street, and played an important role in shaping and developing Boy George's early Culture Club look. 'We all wore Foundry clothes', he comments. 'I wanted us to look like we had a real identity. Sue made me a special outfit, a smock top with matching trousers and shoes all printed with the Star of David. I finished it off with a white Rasta hat made by Stephen Jones.'[34] Dexter Wong, a graduate from Central Saint Martin's, helped to hone the band's collective image. He was responsible for designing one of Boy George's most famous outfits, a smock and matching trousers with a design of printed numbers (above). It was made from a colour-by-numbers bedspread that Boy George found in a toyshop in Spain. As Boy George points out, 'That original Culture Club look, with the numbers printed all over the clothes, was really good, even though somebody said I looked like a rag doll that's had a calendar dumped on his head.'[35] In a well-known photograph by Brian Aris, Boy George, wearing another design by Dexter Wong, parodies this image of himself by posing with a homemade Boy George rag doll given to him by a Japanese fan (opposite).[36]

At the time, Boy George's Hassidic ringlets, Geisha make-up and long flowing robes were regarded as direct challenges to traditional gender conventions. Like Bowie before him, the popular press accused him of cross-dressing or, more precisely, 'gender-bending'.[37] However, for all his sartorial dilettantism, Boy George, as his name suggests, was usually quick to distance himself from the act of drag or transvestism. In Kris Kirk and Ed Heath's *Men in Frocks* (1984), Boy George points out, 'I dress in a similar way to a priest or an archbishop. I wear robes, not dresses, and to be a transvestite you must wear women's clothes. I don't.' He added, 'I'm not fighting an oppressed need to be a woman. I'm proud to be a man.'[38] Certainly, the clothes he wore by Sue Clowes were less inspired by feminine attire than they were by ecclesiastical apparel, or, as Boy George called it 'Catholic camp, religious taboos and ancient symbolism.'[39] Likewise, his smock and matching trousers by Dexter Wong were a version of the long shirt and trousers, known as the *shalwar kameez*, worn by men and women in Pakistan and Northern India. Boy George, like many New Romantics, borrowed elements of dress that were traditionally associated with women, such as long hair and make-up, and incorporated them into his costumes rather than actually dressing to imitate women. Indeed, in juggling with the signifiers of gender, Boy George managed to transcend restrictive definitions of masculinity and femininity.

QUEER

right: **Philip Sallon, London, 1984**
Photograph by Geoff Wilkinson
Styled by Philip Sallon
Courtesy of the *Sunday Mirror*

The New Romantic club scene presented gay and bisexual men with a platform on which they could explore their sexuality. Although Blitz and other New Romantic clubs like 'Hell', 'Le Kilt' and 'Club For Heroes' were not gay per se, their emphasis on individuality and freedom of expression attracted a young, alternative gay crowd. Style innovators such as Steve Strange and Boy George, who both came out as queer in the 1980s, expanded the dress forms visually available to gay men. While even the established gay scene still favoured masculine dress choices, New Romantic dress styles offered validation and acceptance of young gay men's more effeminate inclinations. In adopting skirts and dresses, Strange and Boy George encouraged young gay men to embrace and celebrate their difference and (homo)sexualized identity.

The appropriation of traditionally feminine-associated clothing by gay men in the New Romantic club scene was a bid for visibility. In this respect, comparisons can be drawn with gay rights activists in America during the late 1960s and early 1970s. The Stonewall Riots of June 1969 led to the formation of the Gay Liberation Front (GLF), which set out to achieve equal rights for gay men and lesbians through highly visible demonstrations. The GLF 'created a new language, a new style, a new vocabulary for being gay. It was about being contemporary, about being incredibly, outrageously, exquisitely radical and of course – and most important of all – visible; celebrating being gay rather than living an endless existence codified as "something else".'[40] In what was to become known as 'gender fuck', elements of both male and female dress were worn together in order to confuse the gender signals given by those pieces of clothing.[41] To this end, several members of the GLF adopted skirts and dresses. 'It was the more radical you could get the better, really, during GLF', Justin Stubbings notes. 'So it was lots of bright colours and occasionally chaps in frocks. It wasn't drag, you'd just put a frock on and you'd go out with your boots on. It was all about making a statement and daring, really.'[42]

From the mid-1970s, men in skirts or dresses became a common sight on the more alternative London and New York gay club scenes. Boy George in his autobiography describes his first visit to 'Bangs', a Monday night gay club on Charing Cross Road with his best friend, 'We were transfixed by the demonic horned vision dancing gaily before us … A man in a long black velvet skirt, pit boots, fingerless black leather gloves. His torso was bare, a black Egyptian collar covered his shoulders. He wore black lipstick and mask-like eyeshadow. His hair was shaved at the sides and lacquered up into devil's horns.'[43] It was Philip Sallon, a flamboyant gay figure who played an important role in the formulation of Punk Rock and the New Romantic movement (opposite). Like many gay men, Sallon was attracted to Punk because of its endorsement of difference and individuality. Gay punks developed a style of their own, one that was less severe than that promoted by the likes of the Sex Pistols. It drew more heavily on the androgyny and gender playfulness of Bowie and Alice Cooper and involved 'dressing up, wearing make-up and having "big hair"'.[44] In this respect, gay punk, as typified by Sallon's adoption of skirts, was a continuation of the gender fucking of the GLF and Glam Rock subculture of the early 1970s. Like the members of these two movements, gay punks wanted to shock straight society through their gender-distorted bid for self-expression. Ironically, though, because of their appearance and behaviour, gay punks were usually rejected by both the established gay and punk scenes. Indeed, Philip Sallon was physically thrown out of gay clubs for not conforming to the approved gay images. Sallon, like other gay punks, sought refuge in New Romantic clubs and, later, New Romantic-inspired clubs, perhaps most notably 'Taboo' in Leicester Square, which opened in January 1985.

Taboo attracted a large number of gay men, many of whom came to see its proprietor, the legendary fashion designer and performance artist Leigh Bowery (page 134). The Australian-born Bowery had been invited to host Taboo because of his highly innovative and flamboyant approach to dressing. Bowery dressed as if his life depended on it, wearing a different outfit every week. According to his biographer Sue Tilley, one of his most popular outfits was a short pleated skirt with a glittery, denim, Chanel-style jacket teamed with scab make-up and a cheap, plastic souvenir policeman's hat.[45] However, Bowery's fantastical, carnivalesque costumes often went beyond fashion, occupying an interstitial space between clothing and sculpture. As Paul Gorman notes in *The Look: Adventures In Pop & Rock Fashion* (2001), 'Bowery was all about driving the made-up finery and shock value of the early new romantics that he had read about in Melbourne in

above: **Leigh Bowery, London, c.1984**
Photograph courtesy of David Gwinnutt

right: **David Holah in a skirt by Bodymap, mid-1980s**
Photograph courtesy of Mark Lebon

the early '80s to a logical conclusion, although not many followed the trail he blazed.'[46] Although many may not have followed, many were certainly inspired by Bowery's strange genius, including Bodymap, John Galliano and Vivienne Westwood. David Holah and Stevie Stewart, the designers behind Bodymap, were both regulars at Taboo and huge fans of Bowery's otherworldly costumes. Working with the textile designer Hilde Smith, Holah and Stewart specialized in creating stretch clothes that

had holes in unexpected places (opposite). As Kevin Almond describes, 'Pieces of flesh were amalgamated with pieces of fabric in an effort to explore new areas of the body, previously considered unflattering.'[47] Holah and Stewart's clothes were always for the young, daring and avant-garde and included skirts for men that were modelled on the catwalk by the likes of Bowery and Boy George and the dancer Michael Clark.

From 1985 to 1989 a whole host of new club nights sprang up

in London catering to a mixed gay and straight crowd. In Bill Wilson's words, 'It was very much the post-New Romantic, it was still the same ethos. It was being glamorous, dressing up, looking fantastic, not wanting to look like anyone else ... it didn't particularly matter what sexuality you were ... it was less blatant somehow, but there were a lot of gay people there just expressing themselves.'[48] As part of the androgyny and gender confusion made visible by the New Romantic movement,

skirts and dresses continued to
be worn by gay men as a declaration
of their sexual orientation. Richard
Dyer observes, 'The first time I was
aware of seeing two gay men was
when I came to London and went to
[Steve Strange's club at the Lyceum
Ballroom] The Playground. There
were two men who I thought were
dressed so stylishly. They were
wearing white shirts, black shawl
collared tuxedo jackets with huge
diamante brooches pinned on them,
white socks, black Dr Marten
lace-up shoes and black ankle-length

skirts. They both had amazing
bleached blond quaffed hair.
I remember thinking they looked
fantastic and wishing that I had the
nerve to dress like that at home.'[49]

By the 1990s, however, many
young gay men rejected androgyny
as a means of announcing their
sexual orientation. These men looked
to more stereotypically masculine
self-presentations as a declaration
of their difference and liberation
from straight society. Skirts,
nevertheless, had a role to play here,
too. The kilt, in particular, gained

great popularity, and was worn
by many men as an expression of
hyper-masculinity and a flaunting
of perceived effeminacy. According
to Shaun Cole, the kilt was first
worn publicly by the gay
community at the New York Pride
March in 1993.[50] As The New York
Times noted at the time, the
adoption of the kilt was a reflection
of the masculine ideal, 'the mating
of the masculine, century-old
kilt and the muscular bodies of a
new generation.'[51] Gay men who
wore kilts were adding them to the

left and above: **Gay Pride Parade, London, early 1990s**
Photograph courtesy of Davy Jones

masculinized gay wardrobe that had drawn on utilitarian working clothes since as early as the 1970s.[52] 'Most of the kilts', as *The New York Times* observed, 'were short to show sculpted leg muscles and were balanced with a heavy workboot.'[53] Since the mid-1990s, the kilt has become a standard item in many gay men's wardrobes and is still worn on Gay Pride marches in both England and America (left and above). In Britain, kilts have also become part of the gay, fetish club scene, sold through magazines such as *The Gay Times*. Clone Zone, one of the first explicitly gay companies to sell fetish clothing, offers kilts made from rubber and leather. Andrew Bates, one of the designers behind Clone Zone, points out, 'Our skirts hijack the standard stereotypes – big, hairy, caber-tossing Scots. They are given a macho makeover, either in leather, rubber or camouflage, which has overtures of military discipline and gladiatorial conquests – a fantasy and fetish merger. Even with tongue-in-cheek side-glances at what is masculine, we want men to feel erotic and liberated.'[54]

GRUNGE

Like gay liberationists in America in the early 1970s, many male Grunge 'rockers' adopted dresses as a reactive statement against mainstream society. Grunge emerged out of the late 1980s Seattle music and social scene. It reflected a fusion of Punk and Hippie aesthetics, a synthesis that was culturally-specific to the Northwest coast of America.[55] Its leading protagonists were white, middle-class young men who enjoyed the big riffs of loud, guitar rock but who had difficulty in identifying with its macho and sometimes misogynist posturing. Bands associated with Grunge including Nirvana, Pearl Jam, Mudhoney and Soundgarden, went on to dominate the charts on both sides of the Atlantic during the first half of the 1990s. The music of these bands 'provided an identity and soundtrack for the "lost" Generation X'ers, the (generally) white, middle-class young people who could never hope to maintain, or even want, the same levels of

economic and material achievement of their parents.'[56] In a region that had seen successive waves of liberal, environmentally motivated emigration whilst supporting one of the United States' most virulent white supremacist movements, Grunge was a style that embodied contradictions.

Kurt Cobain, the lead singer of Nirvana was declared the 'spokesman of Generation X'. Cobain's music articulated a wounded, suffering and untrustworthy masculinity. His preoccupation with a pained and vulnerable gender identity was played out in his appearance, most notably in his adoption of baby-doll dresses, often borrowed from the wardrobe of his wife, Courtney Love, then the vocalist of the band Hole (opposite). As Joshua Sims observes:

'Cobain was making a point by wearing them … that being, he was in touch with his feminine side, and/or confused about his identity and who wore the pants

in their family. As crass as it sounds, Cobain's behaviour was indicative of a social malaise affecting a large part of western civilization; because of changing social patterns, men's role in life was becoming unsure, more and more families were dependent upon one (predominantly female) parent. Cobain, like a whole generation of kids born in the late Sixties and early Seventies, was from a broken home and had no father figure to impress upon him the rules of how to act like a man.'[57]

As a father, as a child of divorced parents and as a product of a society with shifting gender roles and expectations, Cobain's appropriation of dowdy floral dresses was both a rejection of traditional family values and an acknowledgement of their power over individuals. Later, Cobain was to adopt the housecoats of suburban housewives, the ultimate symbol of domesticity. By combining baby-doll dresses with heavy workboots, Cobain was also parodying the hard-edged

left: Evan Dando of the Lemonheads, Glastonbury, 1993
Courtesy of Redferns

below: Anna Sui, 'Cyberpunk' collection, Spring/Summer 1994
Photograph by Raoul Gatchalian
Courtesy of Anna Sui

opposite: Kurt Cobain, 1993
Photograph by Steve Double
Courtesy of S.I.N

definitions of gendered dress. It was a look that was pioneered by the 'Riot Grrrls', a highly politicized musical movement that espoused third wave feminism, and which emerged concurrently with Grunge.

Other figures of Grunge also played with this iconography. So-called 'Grunge pin-up' Evan Dando, lead singer of the Lemonheads, wore floral dresses in concert and sang songs from a girl's point of view (page 138). The Lemonheads advocated a less anguished, but no less ambivalent take on the phallic rock god. According to Sims, Dando wore dresses 'in order to show a solidarity with Cobain and impress the girls that he was in touch with his feminine side.'[58] Later, in the nineties, the Smashing Pumpkins, who had been identified with Grunge early in their career, engaged in highly theatrical, stylised cross-gender dressing, which referenced silent and expressionist

films as well as Glam Rock. Pushing the implications of Grunge even closer to the edge, various members of the Punk Funk band Red Hot Chilli Peppers wore dresses, loincloths and miniskirts with tattoos, goatees and heavy eye make-up 'as a brazen invitation for rednecks to challenge their machismo.'[59] With their highly (hetero)sexualised lyrics and athletic performances featuring the lead-singer and guitarist French kissing, they replaced the ambivalence of Grunge with sex-positive cross-dressing. Many Grunge rockers preferred to wear more unproblematically male clothing. In their self-presentation, however, they were driven by the same oppositional tendencies that prompted their more outré icons to adopt dresses. During the conservative Reagan years of the 1980s, and into the 1990s, the dominant American style was that of the Yuppie, whose starched, buttoned-up and designer-clad

bodies captured the aspirational values promoted by mainstream society. As a reaction to and a rejection of 'Yuppiedom', Grunge enthusiasts appropriated the traditional signifiers of blue-collar America, including loose-fitted-jeans, heavy workboots and chequered flannel Pendleton shirts. They advocated 'Dressing Down' at its most extreme, the wearing of oversized clothes often bought from charity, army-surplus and other and second-hand stores. This do-it-yourself approach to fashion reflected the Punk origins of Grunge. Indeed, like Punk, there was a strong asexual element to Grunge, expressed in the trend among men to wear multiple shirts and sweaters around their waists, creating skirt-like flaps reminiscent of the bum-flaps on bondage trousers.

Despite an ingrained anti-corporate stance strongly held by many individuals associated with Grunge, its spectacular

co-option by the mass market has been well documented. That the look of Grunge could be achieved cheaply and with minimal effort did not prevent its adaptation for the catwalk, high street and shopping mall. Grunge style even entered the fashion pages of American *Vogue* in December 1992. In an article entitled 'Grunge & Glory', Jonathan Poneman of the record label Sub Pop urged *Vogue* readers to:[60]

'Throw out your detergent! This is not a call to arms; it's an invitation to dress down and party up! As the fin de siècle draws near, greed has gone to seed. What started out as a serfs' rebellion against aristocratic glamour has turned into a fashion revolution that champions "revolting" for its own sake.'

In a series of photographs taken by Steven Meisel and styled by Grace Coddington, Grunge fashion was (re)presented in a surprisingly authentic and unsanitized manner. Referencing the ubiquitous plaid skirts hanging skirt-like from the waists of Grunge rockers across America, Meisel and Coddington dressed male models in hardy kilts (page 140). The caption that accompanied one of the photographs stated:[61]

'What started as a local, money's-not-an-option style, associated with Seattle's music scene, has turned into an all-American street fashion that mixes rough-and-tumble work clothes with waifish thrift-shop finery – and a generous dose of androgyny.'

In the early to mid-1990s, the layered look of shirts and sweaters wrapped around the waist was re-interpreted by Armani, Versace and Dolce & Gabbana. More recently it featured in Antonio Marras' Spring/Summer 2002 collection (below) . Inspired by Kurt Cobain, Anna Sui created several baby-doll dresses for her Spring/Summer 1994 collection. On the catwalk, they were paired with long johns and chunky boots (page 138). French designer Jean Charles de Castelbajac also took inspiration from the generous housecoats favoured by Cobain. As de Castelbajac comments, 'My dresses for men have a strong sub-cultural element. In the spirit of Kurt Cobain, they are intended to project both strength and fragility. To this end, I chose to use floral fabrics in pastel hues, but then stamped them with various tattoos.'

Fashion designers today continue to be inspired by the skirts worn by the various youth and sub-cultural tribes of the twentieth century. Their adoption by the mainstream diminish their original transgressive potency, but it is part of the deathless cycle out of which new subcultures and new transgressions are born.

left: Photograph by Steven Meisel for American *Vogue*,1992
Styled by Grace Coddington
Courtesy of Steven Meisel/Art+Commerce Anthology

right: Antonio Marras, Spring/Summer 2002
Photograph courtesy of Maria Valentino/ MCV Photo

NOTES

MEN AGAINST TROUSER TYRANNY

1 Aileen Ribeiro, *Fashion in the French Revolution,* London, 1988, p.101
2 Dilys Blum, *Illusion and Reality: Fashion in France 1700-1900,* Houston, 1987, p.18
3 Philippe Séguy, 'Costume in the Age of Napoleon', in Katell le Bourhis *The Age of Napoleon: Costume From Revolution to Empire, 1789-1815,* New York, 1989, p.56
4 Aileen Ribeiro, op.cit., p.94
5 Madeleine Delpierre, *Dress in France in the Eighteenth Century,* New Haven, 1997, p.113
6 Aileen Ribeiro, op.cit., p.104
7 Ibid., p.104
8 Ibid., p.105
9 Ibid., p.105
10 Barbara Burman, 'Better and Brighter Clothes: The Men's Dress Reform Party, 1929-1940', *Journal of Design History,* Volume 8, Number 4, 1995, p.275
11 Joanna Bourke, 'The Great Male Renunciation: Men's Dress Reform in Inter-war Britain', *Journal of Design History,* Volume 9, Number 1, 1996, p31
12 Barbara Burman, op.cit., p.284
13 Ibid., p.277
14 Ibid., p.277
15 Joanna Bourke, op.cit., pp.27-28
16 Eric Gill, Clothes: *An Essay Upon the Nature and Significance of the Natural and Artificial Integuments Worn by Men and Women*, London, 1931, p.195
17 Ibid., pp.187-188
18 Ibid., p.187
19 Elizabeth Hawes, *Fashion is Spinach,* New York, 1938, p.304
20 Ibid., p.305
21 Elizabeth Hawes, *It's Still Spinach,* Boston, 1954, p.37
22 www.kiltmen.com
23 www.amerikilts.com
24 www.amok.ch
25 Ibid
26 Rebecca Arnold, *Fashion, Desire and Anxiety: Image and Morality in the 20th Century,* London, 2001, pp.118-119
27 Ibid., p.121
28 Joel Lobenthal, *Radical Rags: Fashions of the Sixties,* New York, 1990, p.157
29 Peggy Moffitt and William Claxton, *The Rudi Gernreich Book,* Köln, 1999, p.182
30 Jo B. Paoletti and Claudia Brush Kidwell, 'Conclusion', Claudia Brush Kidwell and Valerie Steele, eds., *Men and Women: Dressing the Part,* Washington, 1989, p.161
31 Interview with the author
32 Paul Jobling, *Fashion Spreads: Word and Image in Fashion Photography Since 1980,* Oxford, 1999, p.145
33 Interview with the author
34 Interview with the author
35 *i-D*, July 1984
36 Interview with the author
37 Interview with the author
38 Sean Nixon, *Hard Looks: Masculinities,*

Spectatorship & Contemporary Consumption, New York, 1996, p.181
39 Glenda Bailey, 'Men's Where?', *The Face,* Number 55, November, 1984, p.84
40 Ibid., p.84
41 Nick Logan, 'Myths and Legends', Mitzi Lorenz (ed.), *Buffalo,* London, 2000, p.148
42 Tim Edwards, *Men in the Mirror: Men's Fashion, Masculinity and Consumer Society,* London, 1997, p.82
43 Ibid., p.80
44 Ibid., p.80
45 Ibid., p.83
46 Ibid., p.83
47 Sean Nixon, op.cit., p.204
48 Warren St. John, 'Metrosexuals Come Out', *New York Times,* 22 June, 2003
49 Ibid
50 David Beckham, *Beckham: My World,* London, 2000, p.93

SKIRTS IN HISTORY

1 Philip J Watson, *Costume of Ancient Egypt,* New York, 1987, p.13
2 Rosalind Hall, *Egyptian Textiles,* Buckinghamshire, 2001, p.21
3 Homer, *The Iliad,* New York, 1990, pp.100-1
4 Ethel Abrahams, 'Greek Dress', Marie Johnson, ed., *Ancient Greek Dress,* Chicago, 1964, p.54
5 David J Symons, *Costume of Ancient Greece,* New York, 1987, p.30
6 Bernard Rudofsky, *The Unfashionable Human Body,* New York, 1971, p.269
7 Horatio Greenhough, *Aesthetics at Washington,* Washington, 1851, p.6
8 Lillian Wilson, *The Clothing of the Ancient Romans,* Baltimore, 1938, p.73
9 Larissa Bonfante, 'Introduction', Judith Lynn Sebesta and Larissa Bonfante, *The World of Roman Costume,* Wisconsin, 2001, p.5
10 A.T. Croom, *Roman Clothing and Fashion,* Stroud, 2000, pp.32-3
11 Quintilian, *The Orator's Education,* Donald Russell, ed., Volume V, Books 11-12, Cambridge, 2001, p.157
12 Kelly Olson, 'Matrona and Whore: The Clothing of Women in Roman Antiquity', Valerie Steele, ed., *Fashion Theory: The Journal of Dress, Body & Culture,* Oxford, Volume 6, Issue 4, December 2002, p.390
13 Shelley Stone, 'The Toga: From National to Ceremonial Costume', in Judith Lynn Sebesta and Larissa Bonfante, *The World of Roman Costume,* Wisconsin, 2001, p.17
14 Lillian Wilson, op.cit., p.55
15 Shelley Stone, op.cit., p.16
16 Richard A. Gergel, 'Costume as Geographic Indicator: Barbarians and Prisoners on Cuirassed Statue Breastplates', Judith Lynn Sebesta and Larissa Bonfante, *The World of Roman Costume,* Wisconsin, 2001, p.191

17 François Boucher, *20,000 Years of Fashion: The History of Costume and Personal Adornment,* New York, 1987, p.166
18 Janet Mayo, *A History of Ecclesiastical Dress,* New York, 1984, p.19
19 Ibid., p.28
20 Ibid., p.15
21 Penelope Byrde, *The Male Image: Men's Fashion in England 1300-1790,* London, 1979
22 Ibid., p.57
23 Aileen Ribeiro, *Dress and Morality,* New York, 1986, p.45
24 Penelope Byrde, op.cit., p.59
25 Naomi Tarrant, *The Development of Costume,* London, 1996, p.42
26 Aileen Ribeiro, op.cit., 1986, p.67
27 Ibid
28 Ibid
29 Ibid
30 Norah Waugh, *The Cut of Men's Clothes: 1600-1900,* New York, 1964, p.47
31 Aileen Ribeiro, op.cit., p.87
32 Norah Waugh, op.cit.,1964, p.46
33 Penelope Byrde, op.cit., p.78
34 Ibid., p.102
35 Mark Paytress and Steve Pafford, *Bowie Style,* London, 2000, p.153
36 Norah Waugh, op.cit., p.105
37 Jane Ashelford, The Art of Dress: Clothes and Society 1500-1914, London, 1996, p.277
38 Anthony Burton, *Children's Pleasures: Books, Toys and Games from the Bethnal Green Museum of Childhood,* London, 1996, pp.76-81

EXOTICISM

1 Joanne Entwistle, *The Fashioned Body: Fashion, Dress and Modern Social Theory,* Cambridge, 2000, p.143
2 Malcolm D McLeod, *The Asante,* London, 1981, p.145
3 Venice Lamb, *West African Weaving,* London, 1975, p.16
4 Ibid., p.22
5 Frances Kennett, *Ethnic Dress,* London, 1994, p.85
6 Carol Beckwith and Tepilit Ole Saitoti, *Maasai,* New York, New York, 1980
7 Michael Hitchcock, *Indonesian Textiles,* New York, 1991
8 Mattiebelle Gittinger, *Splendid Symbols: Textiles and Tradition in Indonesia,* Oxford, 1990, p.53
9 Nasreen Askari and Liz Arthur, *Uncut Cloth: Saris, Shawls and Sashes,* London, 1999, p.21
10 Interview with the author
11 Rebecca Arnold, *Fashion, Desire and Anxiety: Image and Morality in the 20th Century,* London, 2001, p.117
12 Interview with the author
13 Interview with the author
14 Interview with the author
15 Interview with the author

NOTES

16 Interview with the author

17 Jean Besancenot, *Costumes of Morocco*, London, 1990, p.139

18 Heather Colyer Ross, *The Art of Arabian Costume: A Saudi Arabian Profile*, Fribourg, 1981, p.41

19 Jean Besancenot, op.cit., p.190

20 Rebecca Arnold, op.cit., pp.27-28

21 Ibid., p.28

22 Joshua Sims, *Rock/Fashion*, London, 1999, p.26

23 Interview with the designer

24 Frances Kennett, op.cit., p.100

25 S. N. Dar, *Costumes of India and Pakistan: A Historical and Cultural Survey,* Bombay, 1969, p.94

26 B. N. Goswamy, *Indian Costumes in the Collection of the Calico Museum of Textiles,* Ahmedabad, 1993, p.136

27 *Arena Homme Plus*, Spring/Summer 1994, Issue 1, p.142

28 Patrick McCarthy, 'The Menswear Revolution', Germano Celant and Harold Koda, *Giorgio Armani*, New York, 2000, p.82

29 Veronica Murphy and Rosemary Crill, *Tie-dyed Textiles of India: Tradition and Trade*, New York, 1991, p.141

30 Jean L. Druesedow, 'In Style: Celebrating Fifty Years of the Costume Institute', *The Metropolitan Museum of Art Bulletin*, Fall 1987, Volume XLV, Number 2, p.20

31 Naomi E. A. Tarrant, 'Lord Sheffield's Banyan', *Costume*, Number 11, 1977, p.94

32 Richard Martin and Harold Koda, *Orientalism: Visions of the East in Western Dress*, New York, 1994, p.17

33 Helen C. Gunsaulus, *Japanese Costume*, Chicago, 1923, 12

34 Farid Chenoune, *A History of Men's Fashion,* Paris, 1993, p.151

KILTS

1 John Telfer Dunbar, *Highland Costume*, Edinburgh, 1977, p.18

2 John Telfer Dunbar, *The Costume of Scotland*, London, 1981, p.30

3 John Telfer Dunbar, *Highland Costume*, pp.24-25

4 James D. Scarlett, *Scotland's Clans and Tartans*, London, 1984, p.40

5 John Telfer Dunbar, *Highland Costume*, p.33.

6 John Telfer Dunbar, *The Costume of Scotland,* pp.69-70

7 Hugh Trevor-Roper, 'The Invention of Tradition: The Highland Tradition of Scotland', in Eric Hobsbawm and Terence Ranger (eds) *The Invention of Tradition*, Cambridge, 1983, p.22

8 Malcolm Chapman, *The Celts: The Construction of a Myth*, London, 1992, p.125

9 John Telfer Dunbar, *The Costume of Scotland*, pp.69-70

10 Hugh Cheape, *Tartan: The Highland Habit*, Edinburgh, 1991, p.32

11 Malcolm Chapman, p.141

12 Ibid., p.140

13 Ibid., p.140

14 Ibid., p.140

15 Lou Taylor, *The Study of Dress History*, Manchester, 2002, p.214

16 Hugh Trevor-Roper, op.cit., p.29

17 Malcolm Chapman, op.cit., p.140

18 Hugh Cheape, op.cit., p.50

19 Ibid., p.52

20 Ibid., p.61

21 Lou Taylor, op.cit., p.220

22 Ibid., p.220

23 Interview with the author

24 Interview with the author

25 Interview with the author

26 Hugh Trevor-Roper, op.cit., p.30

27 Suzy Menkes, *The Windsor Style*, Topsfield, 1987, p.102

28 The Duke of Windsor, *A Family Album*, London, 1960, p.129

29 Interview with the author

30 Interview with the author

31 Interview with the author

32 'John Stephen', National Art and Design Archive, Victoria & Albert Museum

33 Interview with the author

34 Interview with the author

SUBCULTURAL STYLES

1 Shane White and Graham White, *Stylin': African American Expressive Culture from Its Beginnings to the Zoot Suit*, Ithaca, 1998

2 Dick Hebdige, *Subculture: The Meaning of Style,* London, 2001, p.60

3 Mark Paytress and Steve Pafford, *BowieStyle*, London, 2000, p.62

4 Joshua Sims, *Rock/Fashion*, London, 1999, p.114

5 Ibid., p.116

6 Mark Paytress and Steve Pafford, op.cit., p.35

7 Cameron Crowe, 'Playboy Interview: David Bowie', *Playboy*, vol. 23, no. 9, September 1976, p.58

8 Joshua Sims, op.cit., p.116

9 *The Face*, July 1999, p.38

10 Mark Paytress and Steve Pafford, op.cit., p.62

11 Ibid., p.62

12 Joshua Sims, op.cit., p.116

13 Henry Edwards and Tony Zanetta, *Stardust: The David Bowie Story*, New York, 1986, p.107

14 Dick Hebdige, op.cit., p.61

15 Zeshu Takamura, *Roots Of Street Style*, Tokyo, 1997, p.141

16 Dick Hebdige, op.cit., p.63

17 Ibid., p.63

18 Ted Polhemus, *Street Style: From Sidewalk To Catwalk*, London, 1994, p.90

19 Dick Hebdige, op.cit., p.107

20 Jane Mulvagh, *Vivienne Westwood: An Unfashionable Life*, London, 1998, pp.102-3

21 Ibid., p.104

22 Paul Burgess and Alan Parker, *Satellite*, London, 1999, p.25

23 Ted Polhemus, op.cit., p.95

24 Boy George, *Take It Like A Man*, London, 1995, 117

25 Steve Strange, *Blitzed!*, London, 2002, p.43

26 Ibid., p.44

27 Ted Polhemus, op.cit., p.96

28 Boy George, op.cit., p.117

29 Steve Strange, op.cit., p.46

30 Ibid., p.46

31 Ted Polhemus, op.cit., p.96

32 Rebecca Arnold, *Fashion, Desire and Anxiety: Image and Morality in the 20th Century*, London, 2001, p.116

33 Steve Strange, op.cit., p.55

34 Boy George, op.cit., p.164

35 Paul Gorman, *The Look: Adventures In Pop & Rock Fashion,* London, 2001, pp.154-5

36 *The Fashion Book*, London, 1998, p.72

37 Caroline Evans and Minna Thornton, *Women & Fashion: A New Look,* London, 1989, pp.48-50

38 Kris Kirk and Ed Heath, *Men in Frocks*, London, 1984, p.112

39 Boy George, op.cit., p.160

40 Hugh David, *On Queer Street: A Social History of British Homosexuality 1895-1995*, London, 1997, p.228

41 Shaun Cole, 'Don We Now Our Gay Apparel': Gay Men's Dress in the Twentieth Century,* Oxford, 2000, p.88

42 Ibid., p.88

43 Boy George, op.cit., p.73

44 Shaun Cole, op.cit., p.148

45 Sue Tilley, *Leigh Bowery: The Life and Times of an Icon*, London, 1997, p.57

46 Paul Gorman, op.cit., p.165

47 Richard Martin, ed., *The St. James Fashion Encyclopedia: A Survey of Style from 1945 to the Present*, Detroit, 1997, p.53

48 Shaun Cole, op.cit., p.164

49 Ibid., p.165

50 Amy de la Haye and Cathie Dingwall, *Surfers, Soulies, Skinheads & Skaters: Subcultural Style from the Forties to the Nineties,* London, 1996, no pagination

51 'Men in Skirts', *The New York Times*, 4 July 1993, p.3

52 Shaun Cole, op.cit., p.187

53 'Men in Skirts', *The New York Times*, 4 July 1993, p.3

54 Interview with the author.

55 Ted Polhemus, op.cit., p.123

56 Amy de la Haye and Cathie Dingwall, no pagination

57 Joshua Sims, op.cit., p.136

58 Ibid., p.136

59 Ibid., p.136

60 Jonathan Poneman, 'Grunge & Glory', American *Vogue*, December 1992, p.254

61 Ibid. p.254

62 Interview with the author

BIBLIOGRAPHY

Rebecca Arnold, *Fashion, Desire and Anxiety: Image and Morality in the 20th Century*, (London, 2001)

Nasreen Askari and Liz Arthur, *Uncut Cloth: Saris, Shawls and Sashes,* (London, 1999)

S. N. Dar, *Costumes of India and Pakistan: A Historical and Cultural Survey*, (Bombay, 1969)

Jean Besancenot, *Costumes of Morocco*, (London, 1990)

Joanna Bourke, 'The Great Male Renunciation: Men's Dress Reform in Inter-war Britain', *Journal of Design History*, Volume 9, No.1, 1996

Claudia Brush Kidwell and Valerie Steele, eds., *Men and Women: Dressing the Part*, (Washington, 1989)

Barbara Burman, 'Better and Brighter Clothes: The Men's Dress Reform Party, 1929-1940', *Journal of Design History*, Volume 8, No.4, 1995

Penelope Byrde, *The Male Image: Men's Fashion in England 1300-1970*, (London, 1979)

Malcolm Chapman, *The Celts: The Construction of a Myth*, (London, 1992)

Hugh Cheape, *Tartan: The Highland Habit*, (Edinburgh, 1991)

Farid Chenoune, *A History of Men's Fashion*, (Paris, 1993)

Shaun Cole, *'Don We Now Our Gay Apparel': Gay Men's Dress in the Twentieth Century*, (Oxford, 2000)

Susan Conway, *Thai Textiles*, (London, 1992)

A.T. Croom, *Roman Clothing and Fashion*, (Stroud, 2000)

Tim Edwards, *Men in the Mirror: Men's Fashion, Masculinity and Consumer Society*, (London, 1997)

Eric Gill, *Clothes: An Essay Upon the Nature and Significance of the Natural and Artificial Integuments Worn by Men and Women*, (London, 1931)

Mattiebelle Gittinger, *Splendid Symbols: Textiles and Tradition in Indonesia*, (Oxford, 1990)

Rosalind Hall, *Egyptian Textiles*, (Buckinghamshire, 2001)

Dick Hebdige, *Subculture: The Meaning of Style*, (London, 2001)

Michael Hitchcock, *Indonesian Textiles*, (New York, 1991)

Paul Jobling, *Fashion Spreads: Word and Image in Fashion Photography Since 1980*, (Oxford, 1999)

Marie Johnson, ed., *Ancient Greek Dress*, (Chicago, 1964)

Frances Kennett, *Ethnic Dress*, (London, 1994)

Venice Lamb, *West African Weaving*, (London, 1975)

Richard Martin and Harold Koda, *Orientalism: Visions of the East in Western Dress*, (New York, 1994)

Malcolm D. McLeod, *The Asante*, (London, 1981)

Janet Mayo, *A History of Ecclesiastical Dress*, (New York, 1984)

Sean Nixon, *Hard Looks: Masculinities, Spectatorship & Contemporary Consumption*, (New York, 1996)

Ted Polhemus, *Street Style: From Sidewalk To Catwalk*, (London, 1994)

Terence Ranger (eds) *The Invention of Tradition*, (Cambridge, 1983)

Aileen Ribeiro, *Dress and Morality*, (New York, 1986)

–, *Fashion in the French Revolution*, (London, 1988)

Judith Lynn Sebesta and Larissa Bonfante, *The World of Roman Costume*, (Wisconsin, 2001)

Joshua Sims, *Rock/Fashion*, (London, 1999)

Naomi Tarrant, *The Development of Costume*, (Edinburgh, 1994)

Lou Taylor, *The Study of Dress History*, (Manchester, 2002)

John Telfer Dunbar, *Highland Costume*, (Edinburgh, 1977)

Hugh Trevor-Roper, 'The Invention of Tradition: The Highland Tradition of Scotland', in Eric Hobsbawm and Terence Ranger (eds) *The Invention of Tradition*, (Cambridge, 1983)

Gillian Vogelsang-Eastwood, *Pharaonic Egyptian Clothing*, (Leiden, 1993)

Norah Waugh, *The Cut of Men's Clothes: 1600-1900*, (New York, 1964)

Lillian Wilson, *The Clothing of the Ancient Romans*, (Baltimore, 1938)